SECOND EDITION

EARTH-WISE

A BIBLICAL RESPONSE TO ENVIRONMENTAL ISSUES

Calvin B. DeWitt

FAITH
ALIVE®
Christian Resources

Grand Rapids, Michigan

Cover design: Jill Rozmarek

We welcome your comments. Call us at 1-800-333-8300 or e-mail us at www.faithaliveresources.org.

Library of Congress Cataloging-in-Publication Data

DeWitt, Calvin B.
    Earth-wise: a biblical response to environmental issues/Calvin B. DeWitt—2nd ed. p. cm.
    ISBN 978-1-59255-414-0 (alk. paper)
    1. Human ecology—Religious aspects—Christianity. 2. Nature—Religious aspects—Christinity.
    3. Human ecology—Biblical teaching. 4. Nature—Biblical teaching. I. Title.
    BT695.5.D49 2007
    261.8'8—dc22
               2007036816

10 9 8 7 6 5 4 3 2 1

Contents

Epigraph

The earth was given to man, with this condition, that he should occupy himself in its cultivation. . . . The custody of the garden was given in charge to Adam, to show that we possess the things which God has committed to our hands, on the condition that, being content with the frugal and moderate use of them, we should take care of what shall remain. Let him who possesses a field, so partake of its yearly fruits, that he may not suffer the ground to be injured by his negligence, but let him endeavor to hand it down to posterity as he received it, or even better cultivated. Let him so feed on its fruits, that he neither dissipates it by luxury, nor permits it to be marred or ruined by neglect. Moreover, that this economy, and this diligence, with respect to those good things which God has given us to enjoy, may flourish among us; let everyone regard himself as the steward of God in all things which he possesses. Then he will neither conduct himself dissolutely, nor corrupt by abuse those things which God requires to be preserved.

—John Calvin on Genesis 2:15; Commentary on Genesis, *1554.*

Foreword

Though he probably has not known this, Calvin DeWitt has been my mentor. I have wanted to make a difference with my life. I have wanted to make a servant's impact for God upon all his creation. And for that I have needed great teachers.

Cal DeWitt has everything to recommend him as a great teacher. He has advanced training in the sciences of which he speaks. He has studied Scripture with his heart and soul as well as his mind. Cal is also respected highly by his peers. He is a cofounder of the leading evangelical network on the environment (Evangelical Environmental Network), and he was the founding director of an institute for environmental studies (AuSable Institute). Cal is personally intrigued and delighted by God's creation—and has been so from his boyhood. His students revere him not only for his knowledge but also for his integrity. And, besides all that, Cal's work is fun to read.

That's what else I needed: a good textbook. I entered into the advocacy of creation care through the recommendation of other evangelical leaders. I did not know much about the field, but I love to study. I am a pastor, so I was not reading just for me but also for thousands who listen to me. Therefore, I had to be very careful about my reference material. Dr. DeWitt to my rescue! I read *Earth-Wise* as one of my resource books, and I thought, "How could I have missed this as an important part of following and worshiping God?"

I challenge you to learn from Cal DeWitt (with me), and we will benefit others together. The care of God's creation is not just a way to honor the Creator, although it is that. The care of God's creation is not just a way to love your neighbor (and grandchildren) as you love yourself, although it is that too. The care of God's creation is not just another way to obey God's command to cultivate and keep the earth, though it is also that too. The care of creation is a crucial issue. The way we address it could mean life or death for millions of people around the world. We can help protect those least able to cope with environmental degradation. They are among the "least of these" whom Jesus specifically taught about in Matthew 25.

So this is more than a textbook, and Cal DeWitt is more than a teacher. This is a book of life and a book of love. This is a book that will make your life count more for the benefit of others. This is a book that will help you love the natural world that fascinated you as a child. This is a book that will help you love your neighbor in a practical way.

Read this book and you will be different. So will the world.

— Dr. Joel C. Hunter
Senior Pastor, Northland—A Church Distributed
Orlando, Florida

Editor's note: Currently serving on the board of directors of the National Association of Evangelicals, Joel Hunter has helped raise awareness of environmental concerns through his work for the Evangelical Climate Initiative, through preaching and speaking engagements and media interviews, and in his book *Right Wing, Wrong Bird: Why the Tactics of the Religious Right Won't Fly with Most Conservative Christians* (2006), re-released as *A New Kind of Conservative* (Regal Books/ Gospel Light/CBD, 2008).

Introduction

Ihave been in love with the Creator since my childhood and have been inspired and awed by God's creation for more than half a century. I gained an early appreciation for God's creatures from caring for and keeping animals in the backyard zoo of my childhood and youth.

I am a teacher, and I love to teach about the wonders of the beautiful life that envelops the earth. From my first teaching assignment at age 16—a course in herpetology for young people at the Grand Rapids (Mich.) Public Museum—I went on to teach thousands of college and university students (and nearly every other person I've ever met), helping them to develop a sense of awe and wonder for God's world. Like the great Teacher—my model—I too like to teach on field trips! And I am a continuous student, learning from the "university of creation" and from God's holy Word.

One Sunday evening when I was in my teens, I overheard my uncle ask my dad a question about me: "Shouldn't you help Cal do something more important than this—something that will help him get a job?" My dad was guiding him down the basement stairs to see my birds and fish while my mom and aunt prepared after-church coffee and goodies in the kitchen above. As they approached the door to my aviary and aquaria, I heard my dad softly reply that he thought I was doing just fine. You see, my dad had told me earlier to keep doing what I loved to do; that would mean I would do it very well—and that meant eventually someone would even pay me for it. In this—his rendition of Matthew 6:33—he proved to be ever so right! I now get paid for what I love to do. My profession is caring for God's creation and helping others to do so.

From the subtitle *A Biblical Response to Environmental Issues*, it would seem reasonable to conclude that this book is rooted in "the environment." But my own vocation—and "where I'm coming from"—stems from a time before anyone heard or taught much about "the environment" or "environmentalism." So is this an "environmental" book? Yes, and no. While it is a response to environmental issues, its *root*—and the *root* of my vocation—comes from my delight in God's creation. My motivation is summed up pretty well by Psalm 111:2: "Great are the works of the Lord; they are pondered by all who delight in them." What a wonderful world God has given us! It's a world so convicting of God's divinity and everlasting power that everyone is left without an excuse for not knowing something about God from

9

his delightful creation (Rom. 1:20). Our delight calls for our study, our seeking out, and our full investigation of this marvelous creation!

This book aims both to lighten the load we carry and to urge us to joyful, redeeming action in and with God's amazing world. It will not pile on guilt. God knows that we, along with the rest of humanity, are guilty, "for all have sinned and fall short of the glory of God" (Rom. 3:23). But ours is not to grovel in polluted gutters or to wring our hands over our sins. Instead, we are called to go about reclaiming creation for our Lord, knowing that "the earth is the LORD's, and everything in it" (Ps. 24:1) and that we may eagerly do so out of joyful gratitude for God's great gift of salvation.

Even as we begin, we are uplifted by the knowledge of God's rule, of God's loving gift of Jesus—through whom the world was made and in whom "all things hold together" (Col. 1:17). Jesus Christ is the one given by God to reconcile all things to himself (Col. 1:20). We know he is the one we must follow. Jesus is our best example of practicing dominion and stewardship.

So let's join together, not only to explore the dark recesses of creation's degradations but also to resurface into the Bible's teachings on creation's care and keeping—and then to ascend into joyful stewardship of the faithful children of God!

—Calvin B. ("Cal") DeWitt

ONE

Seven Provisions for Creation[1]

I was born and raised in the city of Grand Rapids, Michigan, and for more than thirty-five years now I have inhabited the Great Waubesa Marsh in Wisconsin.

In many ways it is easier to learn of the workings of God's creation in this wetland ecosystem, but the city of my youth also provided a wonderful place to learn creation's lessons. With my brother and sister I felt the drifting wetness of torrential rains and gentle drizzles as we swung on a suspended canvas swing in the shelter of our front porch. One day a tornado's immense funnel cloud roared menacingly over the roof of the nearby Baxter Laundry. On summer evenings we heard the noisy "zzbbrrraaaaaaaaaaaannnggggg!" of nighthawks breaking the silence of the night sky as they pulled out of their dramatic plunging dives. We also watched bats zig-zagging in flight around our corner streetlight to keep insects in check. And then there was Mrs. Lockhart's Dutchman's-pipe—a climbing vine with heart-shaped leaves—on which pipevine swallowtail caterpillars ate away with her reluctant approval. These caterpillars eventually transformed into magnificent butterflies that fluttered around the neighborhood or flopped around as they emerged as captives in my mother's canning jars. Better still were my bike rides to the dump at the edge of town and into the countryside, where I could find frogs, salamanders, snakes, and turtles. I brought home many of these treasures to my backyard zoo where I could study them for hours and days on end.

---

[1]A full treatment of the provisions of the biosphere, in addition to a description of environmental abuses and needed response, can be found in Richard T. Wright and Bernard J. Nebel, *Environmental Science: Toward a Sustainable Future,* 10th edition (Englewood Cliffs, N.J.: Prentice-Hall, 2007).

There was no question in my mind about the reason for all this wonderful life. What I was learning from these beautiful creatures was fully consistent with what I was hearing from sermons in church and from lessons at Baldwin Christian School. All these were God's creatures, works of the Master, the Creator in whom all creatures great and small—his Master-pieces—lived and moved and had their being. They were among the ones we sang about each Sunday: "Praise God . . . all creatures here below!"

Day after day this world opened new lessons about God's creatures and presented new things for which to give God praise. The psalms I sang in church beautifully complemented what I was learning in creation. Remember how Psalm 148 goes, for example? This is the way we sang it:

> Hallelujah, praise Jehovah,
> From the heavens praise His Name;
> Praise Jehovah in the highest,
> All His angels, praise proclaim.
> All His hosts, together praise Him,
> Sun and moon and stars on high;
> Praise Him, O ye heavens of heavens,
> And ye floods above the sky.

And then, in the next stanza:

> Let them praises give Jehovah,
> They were made at His command;
> Them forever He established,
> His decree shall ever stand.
> From the earth, O praise Jehovah,
> All ye seas, ye monsters all,
> Fire and hail and snow and vapors,
> Stormy winds that hear His call.

Then we burst forth with everything we had as we sang of trees, frogs, turtles, elephants, Holsteins, Jerseys, birds, kings, and relatives and neighbors:

> All ye fruitful trees and cedars,
> All ye hills and mountains high,
> Creeping things and beasts and cattle,
> Birds that in the heavens fly,
> Kings of earth, and all ye people,
> Princes great, earth's judges all;
> Praise His Name, young men and maidens,
> Aged men and children small.

Let them praises give Jehovah
For His Name alone is high,
And His glory is exalted,
    And His glory is exalted,
    And His glory is exalted,
Far above the earth and sky.

—Psalter Hymnal, 1959, 1976; 304

Years later on Sunday evenings when friends and neighbors from around our marsh and the nearby city of Madison came together, we often sang that very song. And when we followed our singing with a walk through this wetland, a neighbor shouted, "Birds that in the heavens fly!"

All creation praises God. Of this I am fully convinced. But beyond that, all creation breaks forth with a marvelous testimony—one so powerful that it leaves everyone without excuse for knowing something of God's everlasting power and lordship over all things. I remember in my youth savoring Article 2 of the Belgic Confession because it affirmed, in a deep theological way, the worth of my continuous observation and study of animals and plants in the city, the dump, and the outlying countryside:

Article 2: *The Means by Which We Know God*

We know him by two means:

First, by the creation, preservation, and government
of the universe,
since that universe is before our eyes
like a beautiful book
    in which all creatures,
    great and small,
    are as letters
    to make us ponder
    the invisible things of God:
        his eternal power
        and his divinity,
        as the apostle Paul says in Romans 1:20.

All these things are enough to convict men
and to leave them without excuse.

Second, he makes himself known to us more openly
by his holy and divine Word,
as much as we need in this life,

for his glory
and for the salvation of his own.

I knew from this marvelous confession that reading and study of the Bible in my home, school, and church was very important. And—wonderfully!—this confession also affirmed the importance of reading and studying the "beautiful book" of God's creation.

Today the heavens continue to tell the glory of God, and earth's creatures continue to pour forth their testimony to God's eternal power and divine majesty (see Ps. 19:1-4).

In early spring the Waubesa Marsh bursts forth with extravagant abundance of life. Geese arrive, and soon afterward sandhill cranes wing down, announcing with their clangoring calls the arrival and revival of life on the great marsh.

Why such praise? Why such splendor and rebirth in springtime? A joyful reading of Psalm 104 helps provide the answer. This psalm celebrates God as the great Provider and masterful Creator. God's provisions for life and breath are everywhere evident. God's provisions are so numerous and interwoven with each other that we cannot begin to give them their proper due.

Yet it is vitally important for us to put these provisions of our Creator into perspective. Bringing all this in through our senses and incorporating it into our mind's eye helps us see more clearly God's "eternal power and divine nature" (Rom. 1:20). And through our study we grow to pour more meaning into our singing of doxologies, as in "Praise God . . . all creatures here below!" and "Gloria in excelsis Deo."

Many of us have had awesome experiences in God's creation. Perhaps we have stood at the edge of a great canyon, or at the feet of giant trees in an ancient forest, or in the eye of a great storm. Perhaps we've enjoyed a flowering meadow as the morning mists lifted quietly, and we found ourselves humming "How Great Thou Art." How I wish we could walk together now to a place that would bring forth that song; it would put us into the right frame of mind for understanding God's provisions for creation. Let's open our minds now to the awesome wonder of our Lord's creation!

If at this moment you can put yourself in an environment that calls forth praise to God—do so! Maybe you have a creation-celebrating psalm or recording at your fingertips, or an inspiring view outside your window or in the yard, some flowers on a windowsill, or an open window to let in fresh air. At the very least, shift your position and put your mind in a mood for bringing God praise.

SEVEN PROVISIONS OF THE CREATOR

Let's reflect on seven of God's magnificent provisions for creation. These provisions—many of which are celebrated in Psalm 104—tell something of the remarkable integrity and beauty that have engendered awe, wonder, and respect for the Creator and creation through the ages.

14

Earth's Energy Exchange with the Sun and Space

Our star, the sun, radiates immense energy in all directions, heating whatever is in the path of its rays. This great thermonuclear energy source—the star that brightens earthly life—is a great empowering provision of God's love. It energizes nearly everything we know on earth: green plants and all creatures that eat them, great flows of water and air across the globe, movement of automobiles and aircraft, heating for homes and factories.

Our earth also radiates energy, emitting not visible light but invisible infrared "light"—radiation below the red end of the spectrum. If the heat that earth takes in from the sun is not balanced with heat radiated out by earth into space, the earth's temperature rises. If our earth loses more heat than it gains, it cools. Earth's energy balance—its temperature—needs to be relatively constant for the planet to remain habitable.

Enveloping the earth is its atmosphere. The atmosphere is a protective layer of air situated between us and the sun, and between us and outer space. Among its many functions—like providing the air we breathe—the atmosphere controls energy exchange between the earth and sun and between the earth and outer space. It does this by means of "doorkeeper" gases. Doorkeeper gases—such as carbon dioxide and water vapor—let most of the sun's energy move through the atmosphere to the earth. But these very same gases restrict and delay the flow of energy that the earth radiates into outer space. They do this because they are more transparent to visible light than to infrared radiation. The result is that the earth keeps warm—but not too warm—so that life flourishes. The doorkeeper gases work to make a habitable earth.

Window glass in our cars, homes, and greenhouses works similarly. Such glass lets visible light through to the interior but does not let much infrared radiation out. So the inside of our cars, homes, and greenhouses warms up when the sun shines. Because doorkeeper gases act in a way similar to window glass, they also are called "greenhouse gases." In addition, the effect of greenhouse gases being largely transparent to visible light but not to infrared radiation is called "the greenhouse effect." For our earth, this greenhouse effect results in just the right amount of heat leaving the earth to balance the earth's heat gain from energy coming from the sun. This great provision of God for making the earth habitable by living creatures—including us!—brings joy to our hearts and praise to earth's Maker.

If David or another biblical psalmist had known of this provision, we might have a psalm in our Bible that praises God like this:

> You energize the earth with an outpouring of light;
>> you bathe it with empowering rays.
> You keep the earth warm as with a blanket;
>> you keep its heat near your creatures' hearts.
> Your biosphere flourishes;
>> the earth is full of your creatures.

Not all of the sun's energy supports life, however. It also includes harmful, dangerous, and even deadly radiation—powerful invisible rays above the blue and violet end of the spectrum. Maybe you've seen "black lights" that we can install in some of our electrical light fixtures today. They give off no visible light, but they make light-colored clothing and various minerals appear to "glow in the dark." Such "near ultraviolet" lights produce radiation immediately above the visible end of the spectrum and are not very dangerous. The next higher level of radiation, however—"far ultraviolet"—can be very dangerous. When far ultraviolet radiation is absorbed by living and non-living things, not only does it make them warm up, but it conveys such high levels of energy that it ruptures chemical bonds, breaks molecules apart, and disrupts and destroys living tissues. Of particular concern is the breaking of DNA—the genetic blueprint chemical of living things. Damage and breakup of DNA can result in death to cells and microscopic creatures and can affect the instructions given by DNA in ways that produce skin cancer.

But very little ultraviolet radiation ever reaches the earth—and almost no far ultraviolet! It is intercepted in the atmosphere by a "guardian gas" called *ozone*. Sometimes we experience the sharp smell of ozone produced by arcing electric motors or lightning strikes. This gas can be dangerous for people and other creatures when it occurs in significant quantities near the surface of the earth, and this situation can prompt "ozone alerts" in some large metropolitan areas. In the upper atmosphere, however, ozone is vital; the protective "ozone shield" is another of God's remarkable provisions. If we could collect all the ozone from the upper atmosphere and place it at sea-level atmospheric pressure and at 32 degrees Fahrenheit (0 degrees Celsius), it would be only about one-eighth of an inch (3 mm) thick! And yet that amount of ozone is enough to prevent most of the sun's ultraviolet radiation from penetrating our atmosphere and entering the household of life. That's another reason why God's creatures are able to live on the earth.

If the biblical psalmist had known of this provision by the Creator, we might have a stanza like this in one of the psalms:

> The creatures that dwell in the shelter of God's providence
> rest in the shadow of the Almighty.
> God covers his earth with a protective shield;
> God guards the life he has made to inhabit the earth.
> How great are your provisions, O Lord!
> You so love your world that you protect its life!

Soil Building

Soils build and develop. We learn something of this from gardening, in which we spade plants back into the soil and add compost to make it richer. This process also takes place naturally in fields, forests, and wetlands as organic plant and animal matter decomposes and accumulates. In addition, soil is produced and enriched by the weathering of rocks and grains of sand.

Soil gets richer and more supportive of life as it responds through time to climate, rainfall, and the myriad organisms that live in it. Topsoil builds up, becoming richer in nutrients and more supportive of plant life. Various remarkable cycles are involved in this development: the carbon cycle, the water cycle, the nitrogen cycle—to name just a few. These cycles contribute to a veritable symphony of processes that bring bare landscapes—even bare rock—eventually to support a rich and diverse fabric of living things.

Soil building teaches patience. It can take a hundred years to form an inch (2.5 cm) of topsoil—and yet more often only an eighth-inch (3 mm) of soil is produced in that amount of time! The dynamic fabric of roots, soil organisms, and soils that bind together the surface of the biosphere makes one stand in awe of God's patience as Provider. For "with the Lord a day is like a thousand years, and a thousand years are like a day" (2 Pet. 3:8).

Where does this soil building happen? Everywhere! In the cool of temperate zones, this soil building produces our prairie and woodland soils. Farther toward the north pole it produces the soils of our boreal forests. And in the tropics it produces reddish laterite soils—rich in iron oxides and aluminum hydroxide from the weathering of rocks. All around the world the land is nurtured, refreshed, and renewed.

Soil building helps to hold the whole world together. It helps support creation's integrity by renewing the face of the earth. It is yet another God-given provision, an expression of God's bountiful care for the world. If in 1923 Thomas Chisholm had wanted to include this (and the next) provision in his famous hymn about God's faithfulness, he might have written something like this:

> Summer and winter and springtime and harvest,
>   sun, moon, and stars in their courses above
> join with all nature in manifold witness
>   to thy great faithfulness, mercy, and love.
> Air and all elements, marvelously cycling,
>   tuned to the will of thy most loving grace,
> Building earth's soils and supporting thy creatures
>   steeped in thy love across earth's wondrous face.

> —adapted from "Great Is Thy Faithfulness,"
> Psalter Hymnal, 1987, 1988; 556

Cycling and Recycling in the Biosphere

Recycling is not a recent invention. It is part and parcel of the way the world works. The whole creation uses, reuses, and uses again the various substances contained in soil, water, and air for maintaining its living and nonliving fabric.

The Carbon Cycle. Carbon is the basic raw material from which the carbon-based stuff of life is made. Even as you read this book, you're contributing to the process of recycling this remarkable substance. As every living thing—whether human, raccoon, lizard, or gnat—breathes out, carbon dioxide enters the atmosphere. This in turn is taken up by green plants to remake the carbon-based raw material of life that again is transferred to animals and microscopic life that depend on it for food. And sooner or later these consuming creatures return the carbon to the atmosphere as they again breathe out carbon dioxide or as they die and decay.

The Hydrologic Cycle. Water too is cycled and recycled—in more ways than by our water-treatment facilities.

- Taken up in the bodies of animals, water is released again and again through breathing, sweating, panting, and waste discharge. It then reenters the atmosphere, surface water, and groundwater through natural means as well as through our sewage treatment plants or septic tanks.
- Taken up by the roots of plants, water is pumped up through bundles of tubing in the roots, stems, and leaves of plants and evaporated or transpired back into the atmosphere. Other water taken up by plants is used together with carbon dioxide to make the stuff of life that, after use by plants and animals as building materials and fuels, is again returned to the atmosphere, surface water, and groundwater.
- The water that goes into the atmosphere from plants, animals, and people joins water evaporated from lakes, streams, soil, and other surfaces. This water eventually forms dew, rain, sleet, or snow that again waters the face of the earth. Some of this water is stored in packs of snow high in the mountains, or in glaciers great and small, that in time will slowly melt and run down to streams and rivers below. Still other quantities of this water are stored in wetlands that will also in time slowly discharge water during times of drought. Other water from rain, sleet, or snow runs off to streams and other surface waters to evaporate to form clouds again. Some percolates through the soil back to the roots of plants. Some slips past roots to enter the groundwater to be pumped by wells for human use or to emerge again as springs and eventually to return to the clouds it came from.

As water is evaporated or transpired to the air, almost everything that was dissolved in it is left behind. This sweet distillation expresses God's bountiful love for the world. And the clouds—great condensations of distilled watery vapors—rain down this symbol of God's love again to water the earth. This cycle inspired the writing of Psalm 104, which testifies,

> He makes springs pour water into the ravines;
>> it flows between the mountains.
> They give water to all the beasts of the field;
>> the wild donkeys quench their thirst.
> The birds of the air nest by the waters;

they sing among the branches.
He waters the mountains from his upper chambers;
  the earth is satisfied by the fruit of his work.

—Psalm 104:10-13

Cycles upon cycles . . . cycles within cycles . . . cycles of cycles—the creation is permeated with cycles. Each of these is empowered by energy poured out from the sun; each is empowered by energy poured out through God's Son.

The biosphere—the great big envelope of life that embraces the face of the earth—is what we and all God's creatures inhabit. And all of it relies upon the cycles in creation. The biosphere consists of prairies, oceans, forests, lakes, glades, woodlands, brooks, and marshes. In other words, it is made up of wonderful and highly varied *ecosystems.*

Waubesa Marsh—the great wetland on which I live—is one of these ecosystems. Like every other ecosystem on earth, this marsh has its plants, animals, soils, and climate:

- sandhill cranes whose six-foot wingspans, seventy-year lifespans, and bugling calls seemingly command the great marsh
- iron bacteria whose smallness would escape our notice except for the oil-like film they create over quiet waters
- deep peat soil at the edge of Lake Waubesa, soil that extends to a dizzying depth of 95 feet (29 m) and holds a record of pollens, seeds, and other remains that define its long history
- the ebb and flow of water that comes in from bubbling springs and falling rain—and then leaves again by means of flowing streams, transpiration through the pores of wetland plants, and evaporation from the many land and water surfaces

All of these features and their interactions, and much more, make up the tapestry of the wetland ecosystem. Though it might not seem so at first glance—particularly for many wetlands—ecosystems are places of immense ecological harmony. Not every feature plays the same tune, but in many ways they are all in tune with each other. Each wetland, forest, prairie, lake, and desert is a kind of symphony.

The biosphere is like a symphony of symphonies. In relationship to each other, all plants and creatures and processes great and small contribute to the ecosystems of which they are a part, maintaining and sustaining the living fabric of the biosphere. They continue to bring forth life from death, cycling and recycling the basic stuff of creation, all powered by the sun.

Water Purification and Detoxification

Taking a cue from nature, many water treatment plants in our cities purify water by filtering it through beds of sand in a process called *percolation.* Water that perco-

19

lates naturally through the soil is purified in the same way, but usually over greater distances through soil and rock to the groundwater below. By the time it joins with groundwater that we can pump up to our homes from wells, this percolated water is usually fit to drink. This same purified water eventually also emerges from springs that feed wetlands, lakes, and streams.

As noted in the earlier description of the hydrologic cycle, purified water is returned to the air by evaporation from the surfaces of water, land, and organisms, and from transpiration through the pores of leaves. We call this process *evapotranspiration*, or simply *ET*. ET from plants around the globe is essential for returning water to the atmosphere.

Flowing waters and their living inhabitants also serve as water purifiers. Normal levels of nutrients that enter streams from the land are processed by stream life. If not overloaded, this "ecosystem service" is another of God's important provisions that serves the biosphere well.

In addition, wetlands of many kinds across the globe act as water purification systems. Wetland plants filter out eroded soil carried by moving water and draw dissolved chemicals out of the water as they take up nutrients for growth. Mercury and other toxic heavy metals, for example, are taken up by wetlands and stored in the peat soils they form below. The result is that wetlands produce clear water for rivers and streams, thus keeping flowing waters and lakes habitable. Water clarity allows sunlight to reach aquatic plants, and water purification allows for fish and other aquatic life to flourish.

There is wonder in all of this! God remarkably provides for the production of pure water in nature. Contaminated again and again by sediments and dissolved substances, water is made pure again and again . . . and again!

Fruitfulness and Abundant Life
The whole creation is blessed with fruitfulness and abundant life! The home we call the biosphere is woven into a beautiful fabric of life that envelops earth. This fabric includes 250,000 species of flowering plants—orchids, grasses, daisies, maples, sedges, lilies—in amazingly colorful abundance and beauty. All of these interrelate with water, soil, air, and numerous organisms as they live interdependently and yet in their own distinctive ways. Beyond these are another quarter million species, and many more beyond that—all connected in a web of intricate dynamic interrelationships.

Millions of Fruitful Species. When I was in the ninth grade, I learned that there were about a million different kinds of living creatures. By the time I was in graduate school, I was taught that there were about 5 million species. Scientists today estimate that there may be up to 40 million species of living things on earth! The biodiversity of earth is so great that we are only just beginning to name its creatures. So far we have named only about 1.5 million species.

It is difficult to convey my utter amazement at the seemingly infinite variety of life on earth. I'm even more amazed that despite the dangers nearly every species faces as it goes through its life cycle, most species persist generation after generation, reproducing according to their kinds. Even in naturally occurring shifts in climate, landscape, forest cover, and other environmental surroundings, species persist from generation to generation because they can adapt to changing conditions. Each generation even has its own variety—hardly any two offspring are exactly alike. Such variety produces individuals that are endowed to adapt to new and unanticipated changes in their environment. God not only provides for each species to continue into future generations but also gives each one the blessed adaptability to flourish in new and changing situations. In other words, life not only persists—it flourishes.

Again we can turn to the psalmist to lead us in praise:

> How many are your works, LORD!
> In wisdom you made them all;
> the earth is full of your creatures.
> There is the sea, vast and spacious,
> teeming with creatures beyond number—
> living things both large and small.
> —*Psalm 104:24-25*

I remember vividly a reading of Genesis 1 by Atibisi, an African palynologist (palynology is the study of pollen and tiny plant fragments found in sediments and peat deposits). She sat on the floor with a group of us scientists and theologians in a meeting room in Malaysia prior to deliberations on the status of God's creation and our stewardship. She recited this passage with awesome wonder and God-praising joy. This scientist, who used pollen profiles in layered peat deposits to unravel the earth's record going back to the earliest days of African agriculture, read the passage as an African storyteller. At the conclusion of her reading, this doctor proclaimed, "This is so true; never has there been written a more beautiful and truthful account of the coming of the biological diversity of our Lord's earth. 'God said, "Let the waters bring forth swarms of living creatures, and let birds fly above the earth across the expanse of the sky." . . . And the Lord blessed them and said, "Be fruitful and increase in number and fill the water in the seas, and let the birds increase on the earth"'" (see Gen. 1:20, 22).

God causes the waters to bring forth swarms of creatures, and creation is blessed with fruitfulness. God's blessing is everywhere evident, awesome, and wondrous!

Habitats. Though God likely made special provisions and arrangements for the animals on Noah's ark, that ship would not have been the best place for animals to live out their entire lives. Neither is a zoological park or a botanical garden! Thinking of Noah's ark and zoos and botanical gardens brings to mind the importance of habitats in the life of earth's creatures. The ark needed someone like Noah, a zoo needs a zookeeper, and a botanical garden needs a gardener. But a natural habitat needs none of these—only the sustaining provision of the Lord. While a human protector or restorer of habitats can be helpful, habitats are by nature self-sustaining and have existed in some form throughout the histories of the various species present with us on the earth today.

A habitat provides all the requirements needed by a living species to be fruitful and multiply. It allows a species to fulfill its role or "ecological niche" in the biosphere. Remarkably, with the great variety of ecosystems across the face of the earth and through the interrelations of geography, soils, climate, and living creatures, habitats are continuously being sustained and renewed. Often the actions of some species help produce the conditions required by other species. Added to this complexity is flexibility for the requirements of migrating animals. Shorebirds, for example, need a chain of favorable habitats along migration routes that include nesting grounds and—as much as ten thousand miles (16,000 km) away—an over-wintering habitat.

The distribution of living creatures and their habitats around the globe is the subject matter of *biogeography*. The biogeography of a given species is described by the size and distribution of its supportive habitats. Variations in climate, soils, and many other factors produce biogeographic patterns and structure. Tundra habitats, for example, are found near the poles and high in mountains; deserts are often in the rain shadows of mountain ranges; and deciduous forests flourish in the mid-latitudes of the southern and northern hemispheres.

In their remarkable diversity, patterns, and supportive features, habitats are still another of God's bountiful provisions for life on earth. This provision—with its patterned structure now so evident in satellite imagery of the earth—beautifully makes God's glories known.

The Fabric of Energy Relationships. Already we have briefly recognized that our star, the sun, energizes every green plant on earth and all creatures that eat them. The word *trophic* is from a Greek word that means "to nourish," and relationships that transfer nourishing energy from one species to another are called *trophic relationships*. These relationships are extremely important in the networking of living things across the entire world.

Green plants are at the first trophic level, meaning they get their energy directly from the sun. Other parts of God's creation—including us—receive energy indirectly from the sun by eating plants or by eating animals or other organisms that get their energy from plants. Rabbits are at trophic level 2 because they eat only plants. Bald eagles are at a higher trophic level because they eat fish that eat either plants or other things that eat plants. Everything that is not a green plant depends on eating living things for its energy. God's creatures produce and consume, multiply and diminish, develop and decompose, each depending directly or indirectly on the sun's light and each having a particular role in sustaining biospheric integrity.

Why must the plants be green? Because they contain green chlorophyll and are thus the only organisms on earth that can engage in the remarkable process of photosynthesis. Photosynthesis, the foundation of trophic relationships, is the means by which the sun's energy is captured by green plants for the benefit of all other living things on earth. Energy is the "currency" of creation's economy, and photosynthesis undergirds the trophic fabric that interlaces all of life.

A great provision by God, then, is (again) the sun. Another is photosynthesis, which converts solar energy into a form that plants and other creatures can use. Still another is the meshwork of trophic relationships that provide all earth's creatures the energy they need in order to live, reproduce, and flourish.

We—all creatures great and small—depend on these provisions for life. All of these are God's provisions—for which people pray, lions roar, and ravens cry to God. "The lions roar for their prey and seek their food from God" (Ps. 104:21). And God not only asks Job, "Where were you when I laid the earth's foundation?" but also inquires, "Do you hunt the prey for the lioness and satisfy the hunger of the lions . . . ? Who provides food for the raven when its young cry out to God . . . ?" (Job 38:4, 39,41a). The answer is clear: God is the provider of all these things.

As we focus on these amazing discoveries, our understanding of the symphonies of the biosphere grows. Along with the symphonies of trophic relationships and photosynthesis, there is even the symphony of "peculiar honors" each creature brings to creation's King.

> Jesus shall reign where'er the sun
> Does its successive journeys run;
> His kingdom stretch from shore to shore,
> Till moons shall wax and wane no more.
>
> Let every creature rise and bring
> Peculiar honors to our King,
> Angels descend with songs again
> And earth repeat the loud Amen.
> —*Isaac Watts;* Psalter Hymnal, *1959, 1976; 399*

Global Circulations of Water and Air

Because of its 23½-degree tilt, our earth is unequally heated from season to season. The northern hemisphere gets far more solar radiation in summer than in winter. The opposite is true of the southern hemisphere. Besides these seasonal differences there are, of course, daily differences brought about by the rotation of the earth, which provides night and day, coolness and warmth, in a 24-hour cycle.

These seasonal and daily differences drive the flows of water and air from place to place. Constraining and shaping these flows, however, are land masses, ridges,

23

valleys, and mountain ranges—both above and below sea level. These wonderful movements of water and air combine with all other symphonies in the biosphere to sustain life on earth.

As water and air circulate around the globe, they transport many different things such as carbon dioxide produced by animal and plant respiration, oxygen produced by photosynthesis, and water vapor breathed out by earth's creatures and evaporated from moist and wet surfaces. Carbon dioxide produced by animal and plant respiration is moved and mixed in the atmosphere in ways that bring it into contact with plants. Then plants take up this vital gas to use it in building the carbon backbone of all plant life and the animals that feed on it. Oxygen produced by photosynthesis is similarly circulated by air and water to supply vital respiration and energy conversion for animals and plants.

Global circulations are also vital movers of water vapor. The water put into the air by ET and evaporation rises to form clouds that in turn blow across land and sea to bring water to other places as rain, sleet, or snow. Global circulations are the ventilation system of the biosphere. Global circulations provide the "breath of life" on a planetary scale and are vital to the watering of God's great "garden"—the intricately interwoven fabric of life that covers the earth.

If biblical psalmists had known of these global circulations and of creation's dependence on them, we might have had a psalm in our Bible that went something like this:

> You refresh the creatures with vital breath;
> you bathe your works in winds of life.
> Your providence is everlasting.
> Pastures green breathe life to flocks,
> to which your sheep return their wind.
> Creation is securely held by your grace.
> You ventilate the land and aerate your creatures.
> Your blowing renews the face of the earth.

Human Ability to Learn from Creation

God endowed us human beings with the ability to learn from creation. The precious gift of being able to learn from the "beautiful book" of nature gives us the ability to observe, behold, investigate, and record in our mind's eye what we see, feel, hear, and smell. The images and ideas that then take shape in our minds help us plan and do our work in this world to the glory of our Creator. The learning we gain is also continually tested against our experience. We learn from our mistakes, learn from others whose observations and experiments we trust, and revise our models of the world to better represent the reality of the creation we live in.

This ability to learn from creation comes from God. A 1975 study of the Hanunoo tribe in the Philippine Islands, for example, found that an average adult from the tribe could identify 1,600 different species—all without the help of modern science. These people had knowledge of some 400 more plant species than were previously recorded in a modern systematic botanical survey. What's more, they also knew how to use these plants for food, construction, crafts, and medicine. And they knew where to find all of them—they knew the plants' habitats and their ecology. Studies have produced similar findings in other areas of the world, such as Nigeria.[2]

The ability to build mental models of all aspects of creation—from atoms to plants to habitats to the cosmos—is essential for meaningful human life. These models are nurtured and often refined by our human culture, which is also a gift from God. Early in life we learned the warmth of our family's love, and we grew with love for our Creator as we learned about life in our community, school, and church family. We now continue enjoying these blessings daily as we also learn in our vocations and from the people and other communities around us.

Along the way we are also often "re-minded" by persons and situations. We may be called to reevaluate what we hold in our minds to be true. When presented with concrete evidence or convincing arguments, we might even change our minds. In divine providence our minds are informed, cultured, and cultivated by God's world and God's Word.

People who read God's Word are "re-minded" that "the earth is the LORD's, and everything in it" (Ps. 24:1). They are cultured by the teachings of the Bible to learn of the One through whom all things were made, all things hold together, and all things are reconciled to God (Col. 1:15-20). More than that, believers in Christ are encouraged to be like-minded with Jesus Christ, who reconciles all creation to its Creator. Learning to adopt the mind of the Creator, Sustainer, and Reconciler is a joy and task that lasts a lifetime. The Christian culture with which we are infused therefore prays,

> May the mind of Christ, my Savior,
> live in me from day to day,
> by his love and power controlling
> all I do and say.
>
> —*Kate B. Wilkinson;* Psalter Hymnal, *1987; 291*

What does it mean to have the mind of Christ, of whom it is written:

> The Son is the image of the invisible God, the firstborn over all
> creation. For in him all things were created: things in heaven and
> on earth, visible and invisible, whether thrones or powers or rul-
> ers or authorities; all things have been created through him and
> for him. He is before all things, and in him all things hold togeth-
> er. And he is the head of the body, the church; he is the beginning

---

[2]Awa, N. "Participation and Indigenous Knowledge in Rural Development." *Knowledge* 10:304-316, 1989.

and the firstborn from among the dead, so that in everything he might have the supremacy. For God was pleased to have all his fullness dwell in him, and through him to reconcile to himself all things, whether things on earth or things in heaven, by making peace through his blood, shed on the cross.

—*Colossians 1:15-20*

The Creator, in providing for all people, has given us minds and cultural worldviews that allow us to imagine and learn how the world works. We human beings have been given the ability to know God from his created world and from his Word, and to act on that knowledge. This provision of God allows for the adoption of the mind of Christ. This means that we not only learn from creation but also engage in its care, keeping, and reconciliation in harmony with God's love for the world.

Suggestions for Group Session

GETTING STARTED

The busy pace of modern life easily distracts us from looking closely at God's provisions for us and for the rest of creation. Many of us get so fully occupied on the treadmill of busyness that we have little time to reflect on God's amazing gifts. The air we breathe, the rain that waters the land, the new life that breaks forth from tiny seeds—often we take all this for granted. We might never take time to think of the wheat plants whose fruit we enjoy every day, or of the remarkable beauty of the leaves we enjoy in our salads, or of why we never have to rake the leaves that fall in the forest. The greatest gifts are free. God pours out these gifts to each of us—and to all creation—every day and hour. This chapter celebrates these gifts.

Opening

If you are meeting as a group for the first time, begin by each mentioning a part of God's creation for which you are especially thankful. If you wish, describe a recent experience in which you've particularly enjoyed some aspect of the creation, large or small.

Then you might enjoy reading these words from *Our World Belongs to God* (st. 9):

> God formed the land, the sky, and the seas,
> making the earth a fitting home
> for the plants, animals,
> and humans he created.
> The world was filled with color, beauty, and variety;
> it provided room for

work and play,
worship and service,
love and laughter.

Join together in prayer, thanking God for these and other provisions in creation. Give praise to Jesus Christ as the one through whom all things have been made, hold together, and are reconciled to their Creator (Col. 1:15-20).

To prepare for your discussion of this chapter, you may also wish to read Psalm 104 together.

FOR DISCUSSION

Here are some suggestions for a variety of activities you can do together in your group. You probably won't have time to do them all, so just choose the questions and activities that you think are most appropriate.

From this chapter
1. This chapter describes seven provisions that God has established for creation. Talk about one or two of these that impressed you most. Or maybe one of these provisions surprised or delighted you because you hadn't noticed it before or had forgotten about it. What do these provisions tell us about God?

2. What other provisions has God given us in creation? Try to identify one or two more than the seven identified in this chapter. How many provisions do you think there are? Do you think you could describe them all? Explain. (If you have time, you might tie this discussion in with a reading of some of the poetry in Job 38-41.)

From the Bible
1. Read Romans 1:20. What does this verse say about God's self-revelation in nature?

2. What does Colossians 1:16-17 say about God's continuing care for creation?

3. Read Psalm 19:1-6. What does this passage say about creation's response to God?

From your experience
1. How does God express love for the world? On a large sheet of paper, make a list of all the ways in which God shows love to the world. You may want to divide into small groups of three or four persons to come up with ideas. Think of the teachings of the Bible and about the evidence we see in creation of God's love for the world. Confine your list to the left half of your sheet of paper.

2. How might we image God's love for the world? On the right side of your paper, jot down ideas on how we can act to show God's love and care for creation. Try to pair each idea with a corresponding item in the left column.

CLOSING

In prayer as a group, with various members contributing if they wish, give thanks for God's creation, provisions, love, and care for the world. Conclude with praise to God for sending Jesus Christ, God's one and only Son, our Savior, in whom all things hold together and are reconciled to God (Col. 1:17, 20).

TWO

Seven Degradations of Creation[1]

There was a time when I was oblivious to humanity's abuse of creation. I could always count on finding snakes for my backyard zoo under tar paper and discarded sheet metal at the dump on the edge of town, and bullfrogs and bitterns were always present in the swamps surrounding Reeds Lake. I guess I just thought, as many of us do in our youth, that the world had somehow always been that way.

Many years later, however, while doing my graduate work with my wife, Ruth, on the desert of southern California, I became powerfully aware of the way human beings were abusing creation. It was then that I first became embarrassed by the foolishness of our species. While I was studying the desert iguana—a then-abundant big white lizard that lived in the dry, dusty land at the mouth of Deep Canyon—real-estate developers came to the foot of the San Jacinto Mountains with sprinklers to water the desert surface so it could be shaped with a blade, covered with a slab of concrete, and topped with a house. They were building on a great, gently sloping triangle of land, directing picture windows of air-conditioned living rooms downslope to capture the magnificent view of the desert's grand sweep across the Coachella Valley.

What had formed this great triangle that looked something like a river delta? The summer Ruth and I were there, it had rained only 2.54 inches (6.45 cm), normal for this dry area, so it clearly couldn't be a delta—or could it?

---

[1]A full treatment of the provisions of the biosphere, in addition to a description of environmental abuses and needed response, can be found in Richard T. Wright and Bernard J. Nebel, *Environmental Science: Toward a Sustainable Future,* 10th edition (Englewood Cliffs, N.J.: Prentice-Hall, 2007).

An old prospector who had wandered that desert for decades looking for gold explained: "Nope, it mainly never rains here. But when it does, watch out!" Pointing to the heights of the mountains towering above us, he said, "Once a lifetime or so, up high in them mountains, it thunders and lightnin's, it rains cats and dogs. . . . Floods race down this canyon—spitting sand and rocks and boulders onto the desert below. That's what makes this delta here. Even boulders the size of houses come rollin' down in the ragin' river." Then he lowered his arm and, pointing to a protected point near the edge of the canyon, he said, "Over there, outside the path of the fury, is where the native people camped. They knew what this great delta meant!"

This site where we studied desert lizards would later become Palm Desert, California. Seeds for a city were being planted right in the mouth of a giant river that once a century or so could roll rocks the size of houses down from the canyon above!

Upon traveling back to the area in the 1990s, I found that what once was my study site had become the approach to a drive-in bank. What's more, the owners of the "Gates of the Desert Lodge," which sits in the heart of the habitat of once-abundant white lizards, looked bewildered when I asked about the "big white lizards." With puzzled expressions and bothered disbelief they replied to what they deemed complete nonsense by saying, "Lizards?"

I was now standing in a city. The home of the hundred or so desert iguanas I had studied was now occupied by a bank. Nearby, cattails grew in a roadside ditch—wetland creatures were now thriving here in runoff from overwatered lawns. I did find one big white lizard. It was in the local zoo. And whether they knew it or not, all the people living on this great river delta at the mouth of Deep Canyon were waiting for the next great flood!

No longer am I ignorant of what people are doing in and to God's creation. And while I still sing, "Praise God . . . all creatures here below," it has become more of a hopeful doxology. I hope that God's big white lizards, God's deserts and prairies, and so much more will continue to exist and bring praise to their Maker. I hope that people discover the praise-giving of all creatures. I hope that people take care to learn well about their environmental surroundings so they can live more in harmony with creation, avoiding destruction of important habitats as well as danger for themselves or for the generations that follow.

What is the status of creation today? How are we faring as stewards of God's world? As people entrusted with the care of God's creation, we need to ask these questions, and they are not easy to answer. Answering this question has become part of my professional work, and to the best of my ability I have done a computer search of 700,000 titles of articles on the environment. I have pruned this collection down to those written in the scientific, refereed literature and have organized these into major topics that I call "Seven Degradations of Creation."

Before proceeding with this summary, however, it may help to explain the meaning of "refereed literature." We know how referees are used in sports—they make sure the game is played by the rules. Similarly, refereed literature is read carefully by referees before it is published. Referees are carefully chosen for the depth and breadth of their knowledge, for their discernment and judgment, for their record of fairness, and for being free from the influence of sponsors and spectators.

The editors of refereed or "primary" literature normally use three referees to critically evaluate each article or "paper" (as professional articles usually are called). After reading the paper, the referees make independent and anonymous reports to the editor and recommend whether to "reject," "publish," or "publish with revisions." If the editor gets a mixed review, the paper may be sent to still other qualified referees. If the paper must be revised, each revision is again reviewed by three referees. Articles that pass these reviews are published periodically in professional journals, usually by a professional society to whom the editor is responsible. This highly disciplined procedure is designed to keep us researchers honest about what we know and do not know.

There are two other kinds of environmental literature we should know about: "gray" and "popular" literature.

Gray literature consists of reports from government agencies such as the Environmental Protection Agency, from state departments of natural resources, from colleges and universities, from granting agencies, and from think tanks, institutes, and foundations. This literature also is important, but it is not considered as authoritative because it does not undergo the same kind of disciplined review as does primary literature. Gray literature often uses different standards and is more susceptible to outside influences, and it may have more on its agenda than reporting new knowledge. As a result, it generally is not relied upon by professional researchers for a basic understanding of how the world works and what is happening to it.

Popular literature consists of newspapers, magazines, leaflets, and brochures. Like gray literature, it also is important, but it is not normally considered to be authoritative.

What I present here as "Seven Degradations of Creation" is based on primary or refereed literature. This means I have not gotten my information from government or university reports, newspapers, opinion polls, television talk shows, think tanks, or popular articles. This may mean that what I write about here is less dramatic than what can be read or heard elsewhere, but it will not be boring. Instead, I'm sure you will find that the magnitude of environmental degradation is overwhelming!

SEVEN DEGRADATIONS OF CREATION

Alteration of Earth's Energy Exchange

As we noted in chapter 1, the biosphere relates to the rest of creation through the great gaseous filter of the atmosphere, mainly by the flow of energy between the earth, the sun, and outer space. For a very long time, or so it seemed, human beings could take our atmosphere for granted. We did not understand very well its role in the rhythms of creation. In many ways we probably figured we couldn't change or degrade it. Somehow, it seemed, the atmosphere would always take care of itself as it continued to keep things favorable for life on earth. Today we know we cannot take the atmosphere for granted because we are in the process of changing it—with serious consequences.

It's becoming clearer that instead of seeing creation as "a beautiful book . . . to make us ponder the invisible things of God: his eternal power and his divinity" (Belgic Confession, Art. 2; see Rom. 1:20), many people in our culture in the past couple of generations—including Christians—have tended to shift toward thinking of creation as a "bag of resources" to be used. I remember when I first realized this shift from "book" to "bag." I thought of a library—and how instead of looking at it as a place to learn, people shifted toward seeing it as a collection of things to burn. Natural resources could be gathered and counted, stacked and stored in orderly rows and neat facilities, and then marketed and sold to make money, grow economies, and provide energy not just to meet our needs or to aid us in our work and learning but to feed our insatiable appetites for more . . . and more . . . and more. Often we have done this just to feed our egos or to gain a sense of status. One example of this shift became painfully apparent to me decades later as I stood with a visitor on the great Waubesa Marsh admiring a V-shaped flock of swans flying overhead. My visitor asked, "How many pounds would that big one there dress out at?"

Global Warming. What does all this have to do with our atmosphere? It has to do with our changing the composition of the atmosphere by our grand-scale burning of great deposits of carbon, sequestered beneath us as coal, peat, and oil. It also has to do with carbon being released as carbon dioxide from burning forests and with the opening of carbon-rich soils to the atmosphere for the purposes of agribusiness. Because of these practices, carbon dioxide is increasing every year in our atmosphere—at an increasingly dangerous rate.

As a people, as a culture, and even more as a catalyst in today's worldwide economy, we have overlooked the lessons of the great carbon deposits that have helped make the earth more habitable for ages and ages. And our rapid consumption of these deposits as fuels for our way of life is much like burning library books as fuel instead of reading them for the lessons they can teach.

In distant times past, over eons and eons, great carbon deposits formed because green plants took carbon dioxide from the atmosphere, making the earth more continually habitable for living, breathing creatures. Plants breathed in carbon dioxide gas from the atmosphere and converted it into carbon-based solids that were deposited in peatlands and coal formations. Coral reefs took shape as the carbon-based remains of coral animals formed great deposits of petroleum—"rock oil," named from the root words *petra* ("rock") and *oleum* ("oil").

Today, however, we are burning these deposits—returning their carbon to the atmosphere at thousands of times the rate it took for them to be stored. Recently we have discovered the need to sequester the carbon dioxide produced by our burning of coal, peat, and oil—and most of us are curiously ignorant of the fact that this sequestering had already been accomplished by the wetland and coral life of the earth.

Now we find it surprising that earth's capacity to retain heat is increasing and that global temperatures are rising. But this should not surprise us. In chapter 1 we admired God's provision of the atmosphere with its mix of gases that control the energy "deposits and withdrawals" of our planet. As we increase the volume of carbon dioxide, which functions as a "doorkeeper gas" or "greenhouse gas," the atmosphere is holding in more heat—making the earth a hotter "greenhouse." The result is a warming of the globe.

Earth's temperature has been rising slowly over centuries as evidenced by melting snow caps, receding glaciers, and a slowly rising sea level. But today this rise is accelerating, with consequences not only for earth's temperature but also for the distribution of temperature across the planet. This brings about changes in patterns of rainfall and drought, including an increased capacity of the atmosphere to hold water. And ironically a few places in the world now have cooler temperatures than before.

Depletion of the Ozone Shield. Earth's ozone shield, as we noted in chapter 1, absorbs much of the sun's ultraviolet radiation, protecting life from damage to DNA. Ozone destruction has been under way, however, because of human abuses of creation—particularly through the production of chlorofluorocarbons (CFCs) that until recently were widely used as refrigerants, fire-extinguisher ingredients, hair-spray propellants, and more. Destruction of the ozone shield—now being addressed but in need of careful monitoring—results in more ultraviolet light reaching the earth. Ultraviolet rays kill microscopic creatures on the earth and cause skin cancer in people and animals. Thankfully many policy makers and business executives today have recognized this serious problem, and in an agreement called the Montreal Protocol on Substances that Deplete the Ozone Layer they have begun implementing a program for protecting the ozone shield and are meeting with success.

Soil and Land Degradation

What once was the tallgrass prairie is what we now call the corn belt. In much of this region today two bushels of topsoil are lost for every bushel of corn produced.

Pesticides and herbicides, made available after military chemists developed "peaceful" uses of biocides after World War II, made it possible to plant corn, or any crop, year after year on the same land. Crop rotation—from corn to soybeans to alfalfa hay—and pasturing and fallowing were abandoned. Farmers became "free" to plant the same crop year after year—and often were urged to do so by chemical manufacturers and their salespeople. Farm animals could now be kept in

33

feedlots and confinements that allowed for intensified use of the land. Topsoil lost by resulting wind and water erosion could be compensated for by increasing fertilizer inputs. As a result, soil life has been devastated.

Earthworms no longer inhabit most farmland. The microscopic life of the soil has been severely altered. Birds no longer inhabit former fencerows and hedgerows that once separated fields. Most of the land never rests. Many of the habitats of prairie, grassland, forest, and field creatures have become chemical deserts. Even many domestic creatures are deprived of both a pasture and a pastor.

As we consider this degradation, we might reflect on the meaning of this verse from the Bible: "When you enter the land I am going to give you," says the Lord, "the land itself must observe a sabbath to the LORD" (Lev. 25:2). God warned Moses that if the people did not obey this law, the land would be laid waste. After the land had become a desert, the people would be driven away. Then the land would have the rest it did not have while the people lived on it (Lev. 26:14-17, 32-35).

Consumption, Waste, and Ecosystem Dysfunction

In our day, 70,000 different chemicals are being used in commercial quantities, most of them brand-new to the creation, with about 1,000 more being added each year. Many and perhaps most of these are part of the environment in which we and other organisms live. Yet these are materials that living organisms have not had experience with in the past. Unlike chemicals made by organisms and the earth, some of these chemicals leave living things defenseless. Some are even specifically designed to destroy life: biocides, pesticides, herbicides, avicides, and fungicides. Other materials pose additional problems for living things. For example, oil spills destroy life and habitats and devastate human livelihoods on shores and seas. Mercury from smokestacks rains down on the earth and its creatures.

Every item in our homes, offices, churches, and industries is a reworked part of creation. Every product we make, each housing and commercial development we build, every road we travel alters creation. While knowing this full well, we often neglect to recognize the immense changes that we billions of people bring to the earth. We remove parts of the creation, make products and by-products, and produce discards and wastes.

Consider styrofoam cups as an example. We move oil by ship from Saudi Arabia to chemical plants. There the oil is transformed into *monomers*, which are then transported to factories that mold them into styrofoam cups. These cups are distributed to stores, where we buy them for use in our homes, schools, and churches. After using them once, we discard them into wastebaskets, move them to trash containers, and truck them to landfills. As the cups slowly decompose, their remains liquefy to form leachate, which is either drained off and processed by a sewage plant or leaks into groundwater that may next contaminate springs and wells. As styrofoam decomposes, it also produces carbon dioxide, methane, and other materials that add to greenhouse gases in the atmosphere.

Ours is mainly a flow-through economy. It taps creation's wealth at one point and discards by-products and wastes at another. Nature's economy is cyclical; ecosystems sustain themselves by cycling materials. Our economy threatens creation's economy. We interfere with nature's cycles on a grand scale as we "trash" its creatures, pollute its waters, and mow down its forests and prairies.

As we consider this degradation, we should thoughtfully reflect on this passage from Ezekiel: "Is it not enough for you to feed on the good pasture? Must you also trample the rest of your pasture with your feet? Is it not enough for you to drink clear water? Must you also muddy the rest with your feet?" (Ezek. 34:18).

Land Conversion and Habitat Destruction
Since 1850 people have converted 2.2 billion acres of natural lands for human uses (8.9 million square km, an area slightly smaller than China's total land area of 9.2 million square km). Compare this with earth's 16 billion acres that support some kind of vegetation (a nearly equal area consists of ice, snow, and rock) and a current world cropland of 3.6 billion acres. The conversion of land goes by different names, depending on what is done: it may be called deforestation (of forests), drainage or "reclamation" (of wetlands), irrigation (of arid and semi-arid ecosystems), or opening (of grasslands and prairies). The greatest land conversion under way today is tropical deforestation, which removes about 25 million acres of primary forest each year—an area the size of the state of Indiana.

The immensity of this destruction illustrates humanity's power to alter the face of the earth. Why do we continue with tropical deforestation? Largely because we are *able* to—and because it allows us to enjoy inexpensive products like cheap plywood, bathroom tissue, and packaging for all kinds of things from orange juice to fast-food hamburger meals. All this comes at the cost of destroying the long-term sustainability of soils, forest creatures, and resident people.

In the United States and Canada, woodlots and the habitats they provide are replaced with parking lots, buildings, and additions to homes, offices, and churches. Of the 400 million acres of cropland used for agriculture in the United States, about 3 million acres are converted to urban uses every year. In Canada and the U.S., fields for grazing and crops no longer are "carved" from forests, they *replace* the forests. And housing developments are replacing some of the best cropland.

The Bible speaks to this particular degradation when it says, "Woe to you who add house to house and join field to field till no space is left and you live alone in the land" (Isa. 5:8).

Species Extinctions
There are some 10,000 known bird species, of which one goes extinct each year. (One scientist calls this vanishing of whole species "the death of birth.") Research on habitat destruction predicts that by the end of this century as many as 10 species of birds will go extinct each year. If action is not taken to preserve birds, 12 percent of all known bird species will be extinct by the year 2099. In sizing up the status

35

of creation, a worldwide coordinated effort by scientists produced the Millennium Ecosystem Assessment, stating that if needed action is not taken, 23 percent of mammals, 25 percent of conifers (pines, spruces, and their relatives), and 32 percent of amphibians will be threatened with extinction during this century.

Sylvia Earle, a scientist who leads Conservation International's Global Marine Division, adds the following comment on worldwide industrial fishing: "With 70 percent of the world's coastal fish stocks overexploited or collapsed and 90 percent of the biggest fish wiped out, we have turned to the deep oceans in our increasingly relentless and destructive pursuit of the dwindling supply of seafood." One indication of this is that for our Friday-night fish fries (popular in some regions), the fish no longer come from Cape Cod but from Iceland.

While we have given names to most species of plants and animals in North America and Europe, we have not accomplished that in the tropics. Named or not, however, many of those species appear in our stores, lumber yards, offices, boats, and homes in the form of cheap plywood, furniture, wallets, and shoes. Children around the world are paid pennies to bring in skins of once-living creatures that soon are manufactured into fashion items.

We add to this species destruction when we destroy natural habitats by expanding our homes and churches and eliminating woodlots or wetlands. Even butterflies, once so common in the everyday life of city and country, are losing hold as their habitats are destroyed, their food plants are killed by herbicides, and they themselves are killed by "broad-spectrum" pesticides.

Some ecologists now urge us to plant butterfly gardens as natural "arks" for preserving these creatures. Others urge preservation of remaining woodlots and prairies as natural "arks" in response to what has become a "deluge of people." Even now, some churchyards in England, because they remain largely undisturbed by real-estate development, are the sole remaining habitats for some creatures.

A Scripture verse to ponder as we consider these losses is Genesis 6:19, in which the Lord says to Noah: "You are to bring into the ark two of all living creatures, male and female, to keep them alive with you."

Global Toxification

A major feature of the earth's dynamic weather, ocean, and river systems is their life-sustaining transport and distribution of materials around the globe. Of the thousands of chemical substances people have created, hundreds have been injected into the atmosphere, discharged into rivers and oceans, and leaked into groundwater by means of "disposal" systems and by pollution from our vehicles, homes, chemical agriculture, and industry. Some have joined global circulations, with substances like DDT showing up in Antarctic penguins and biocides appearing in a remote lake on Lake Superior's Isle Royale. Cancer has become pervasive in some herring gull populations. Chemical and oil spills kill creation's life on a massive scale. Globally circulating toxins disrupt ecosystems, and hormone-mimicking chemicals create reproductive disorders and affect normal development in animals and people.

In the interaction between creation's economy and ours, we face a planetary challenge: the consequences of what some call "the rape of the earth." No longer are *local* environments affected only by *local* polluters. Global toxification affects all life: all creatures, great and small; all people, rich and poor.

We need to reflect on the words of Jeremiah 2:7 as we consider what we have done to God's creation: "I brought you into a fertile land to eat its fruit and rich produce," says the Lord; "but you came and defiled my land and made my inheritance detestable."

Human and Cultural Abuse

Among the most severe reductions of creation's richness is degradation and extinction of cultures that have lived peaceably and sustainably on the land for centuries. Many Amish and Mennonite farming communities, for example, operate under severe pressure from increasing land taxes and encroaching urban development. In many cases these pressures compel them to abandon their farms. In the tropics, longstanding cultures living cooperatively with the forest are being wiped off the land by force, death, and legal procedures devised to deprive them of their traditional lands. As these people are run off or extinguished, so is their rich heritage of unwritten knowledge. Successful ways of living in harmony with the land are forgotten, names of otherwise undescribed forest creatures are lost, and information on the uses of a wide array of tropical species for human food, fiber, and medicine is wasted.

Agri*culture* is being displaced by agri*business*. Seeds of a wide variety of plants suited to small farms and gardens are displaced by new strains suited to mechanized planting and harvesting—strains uniform in color, size, and time of ripening. An aggressive economy, seeking to maximize immediate return at the expense of long-term sustainability, is sweeping the globe. The meek people of the earth are displaced by labor-saving technology; the powerless are pushed to the margins of the land or into cities. Disconnected from land that could sustain them, they are driven into joblessness and poverty. In the name of conducting "good" business and making "sound" investments, power brokers deprive powerless people of the ability to take care of themselves and the creation.

God's Word says, "Do not take advantage of each other. . . . The land must not be sold permanently, because the land is mine and you reside in my land" (Lev. 25:17, 23). The Bible also says that the land must be returned to the poor and meek (Lev. 25:28). The Lord observes that "even the stork in the sky knows her appointed seasons, and the dove, the swift and the thrush observe the time of their migration. But my people do not know the requirements of the LORD" (Jer. 8:7).

RESULTS: BIOGEOGRAPHIC AND TROPHIC RESTRUCTURING OF THE BIOSPHERE

What are the big words in this subheading all about? Well, at about the turn of the century a colleague of mine, Professor Steve Bouma-Prediger, asked me to prepare a paper for the *Christian Scholar's Review* on the topic "Just What Is the Status of the Creation?" He gave me about three years to study the question before publishing the paper in 2003. My work already had produced what I have written in the preceding pages, but I was surprised by what I found further, even though discovery about the environment and what we human beings are doing to it are a continuing part of my vocation. Here is what I concluded in that extensive paper:

> Our species, in contrast with every other, affects biospheric dynamics on a grand and pervasive scale. In our day we find, remarkably, that we have become a principal geological force. We find ourselves to have significantly restructured the biosphere both biogeographically and trophically. Climate change now pushes plant and animal ranges 3.8 miles pole-ward each decade, nearly one-third of the earth's arable land has been lost to erosion, biodiversity is seriously threatened by habitat destruction and toxification, and overexploitation has brought collapse of the world's major fisheries and an adverse restructuring of ocean food webs. Earth is now under human domination.[2]

CHOOSING LIFE

Creation's garden abundantly yields blessed fruits, sustainably supporting us and all life in its God-declared goodness. But we descendants of the first Adam have made the choice to extract more and yet more at the expense of destroying creation's protective provisions and blessed fruitfulness. Before this human onslaught fall the earth's creatures. Some have their populations severely diminished, while others are wiped off the face of the Creator's canvas. We often find ourselves among those who have chosen to trash the great gallery of earth's Maker, replacing it with our own creations. These new creations claim to be "for the greatest good" and "bigger than life," surpassing creation itself. Under this arrogant assault on the fabric of the biosphere "the earth dries up and withers. . . . The earth is defiled by its people" (Isa. 24:4-5).

Since the beginning of creation, we human beings have been making choices. Early on, we chose to know good and evil. In the past several centuries many have chosen to redefine the long-recognized vices of avarice and greed as virtues. We have come to believe that "looking out for number one" means getting more and more for ourselves. *Self*-interest, we now profess, is what brings the greatest good. Choices made for the creation, for the Creator, have been usurped by choices made

---

[2]This is a shortened and edited version of the original statement.

for *me* and "the economy." Our world today professes, "Seek first a job (money, success), and all other things will be yours as well" (compare to Matt. 6:33). The biblical view, by contrast, calls us to find our "vocation" in God's creation.

God says through Moses, "I have set before you life and death, blessings and curses. Now choose life, so that you and your children may live and that you may love the LORD your God, listen to his voice, and hold fast to him. For the LORD is your life . . ." (Deut. 30:19-20).

While we are expected to enjoy God's creation and its fruitfulness, we are not granted license to destroy the earth. While human beings are expected to be fruitful, so is the rest of creation: "God said, 'Let the water teem with living creatures, and let birds fly above the earth and across the vault of the sky.' . . . God blessed them and said, 'Be fruitful and increase in number and fill the water in the seas, and let the birds increase on the earth.' . . . 'Let the land produce living creatures according to their kinds, creatures that move along the ground, and wild animals, each according to its kind.' And it was so" (Gen. 1:20-24). Our expansion may not be at the expense of the fruitfulness of the rest of creation.

Suggestions for Group Session

GETTING STARTED

It is easy to go about living without ever thinking about the results of our actions. We frequently "throw things away," never thinking about where "away" is. We spray a substance designed to kill an insect, never wondering whether that substance will kill or hurt other life as well. We decry the destruction of the great trees of California as we chat around our redwood picnic table. We are part of a society that has distanced us from the results of its actions. And the result of all this is that the environment is being degraded. This chapter describes some of the major degradations of creation and helps build an understanding of why we need to be concerned for creation and for future generations.

Scripture Readings

As a group, look up and read the following passages in the order in which they are listed here. What beauties and provisions of creation do these Scriptures describe? In what ways are people called to account for their actions?

Genesis 1:1-5
Jeremiah 4:23
Genesis 1:20-22
Jeremiah 4:25-26
Leviticus 26:27, 32-35
Ezekiel 34:18-19

Opening Prayer

Confess that in our sinfulness we human beings have degraded God's creation. Ask God for forgiveness and for the grace to conduct reconciling works that are worthy of repentance.

FOR DISCUSSION

How do we connect with these degradations of creation?

1. On the left side of a large sheet of paper make a list of the seven degradations of creation noted in this chapter. Then, on the right side of the page, write down how we personally contribute to each of these degradations in our daily lives.

What can we learn by reflecting on our childhood?

2. Think back to something that in your childhood or early youth was a wonderful part of creation but now has been degraded or destroyed. Describe it and what happened to it.

What do we know about the things we buy and where they come from in creation?

3. Identify one item you have purchased in the past week and sketch out or describe on a piece of paper where it originated, how it eventually came to you, and where it ultimately is going. Then discuss the following questions:
   - How far has it traveled?
   - What effects has this item had on creation in the course of its journey?
   - What information is provided on whatever label or information came with this item?

What are the underlying causes of environmental abuse?

4. Invite group members to suggest what they think is the greatest environmental abuse we are facing in today's world. (Various answers may be given.) Then, all together or in small groups of three or four, identify the underlying cause or causes of *all* the abuses you have identified. (If people divided into small groups, have a reporter from each group share its findings with the larger group.) Discuss the main cause or causes of degradation to God's creation and what must be done about it. What does society have to say about it? What does the Bible say? Is addressing this important? Why or why not?

Isn't saving people more important than saving species?

5. Sometimes Christians ask, "Isn't it more important to save people than to save species?" Invite group members to share their initial thoughts. Then refresh yourselves on the story of Noah and the flood in Genesis 6-9. Reflect together by asking questions like these:
   - Why did God save living creatures, according to their kinds (species), as well as people?

- If saving people always is more important than saving species, how might this story have been written?
6. Read John 3:16 and Revelation 11:18. What do these passages tell us about God's love and care for the world as well as its people?

What can I do?
7. Pick one of the seven degradations we have studied in this chapter and describe what we can do about it in our personal lives, church, and community.

Do we and society know the meaning of sin?
8. Douglas John Hall in his book *Imaging God: Dominion as Stewardship* points out that some environmental scientists today who study environmental degradation are helping us rediscover the meaning of sin—and these scientists are not necessarily Christian.
- What do you think—has our society lost a sense of the meaning of sin?
- Have Christians lost a sense of the meaning of sin? If so, in what way? If not, why not?
- How would you describe humanity's abuses of creation to a person who might not know God?

CLOSING

Consider what you have learned about the underlying cause or causes of environmental degradation and what to do about these things. Think through the importance of confession and repentance in connection with abuses of God's creation. Conclude your session with a confessional prayer in which everyone is welcome to participate.

41

THREE

A Biblical Perspective on Creation Care

W e know that over the centuries the Bible has been critically important to people who seek to live in love and obedience to God. The Bible's importance continues today, not only for church and home but also (and this surprises many Christians and non-Christians alike) for the environment. The Bible is hardly a minor contributor on caring for creation. In fact, the Bible provides such powerful environmental teachings that it can be thought of as a kind of ecological handbook on how to live rightly on earth!

Among its many teachings the Bible helps us understand our privilege and responsibility for environmental stewardship—for creation care. The Bible also helps us thoughtfully address who we are, how we have failed to live up to our God-given identity, and the problems we create in creation.

The Bible's serious treatment of environmental matters should not surprise us. Since God creates and sustains all of creation, we should expect the Bible to call us to bring honor to God in creation. We should expect Scripture to support creation's care and keeping and to encourage us to maintain the integrity of the creation that God repeatedly calls "good" (Gen. 1:4, 10, 12, 18, 21, 25, 31). Moreover, since the Bible professes Jesus Christ as the one through whom *all things* are reconciled to God (Col. 1:20), we should expect it to decry creation's destruction, to call for creation's restoration, and to look forward to the whole creation's being made right again. And so it does!

Keeping in mind the degradations we have summarized and being aware that many people today yearn to restore the integrity of creation, it can be helpful to read the Scriptures afresh, searching for their ecological insights on how rightly to live on the earth. The following sections of this chapter identify eight biblical principles that help disclose the Bible's powerful environmental message. No doubt you will be able to identify many other biblical principles as well.

1 THE EARTHKEEPING PRINCIPLE

As the Lord keeps and sustains us, so we must keep and sustain our Lord's creation.

Genesis 2:15 conveys a marvelous teaching. Adam is expected by God to *serve* the garden and to *keep* it.

The Hebrew word for *serve* (*'abad*) is translated as "till," "dress," and "work" in some recent versions of the Bible. But "serve" is also a possible translation, as in *Young's Literal Translation of the Bible*. God expected Adam and his descendants to meet the needs of the garden of creation so that it would persist and flourish. But how can we *serve* creation today? This certainly is a puzzle we can discuss with our friends. (We'll talk more about this when we discuss "The Con-Servancy Principle" later in this chapter.)

God also expected Adam and his descendants to *keep* the garden. The word for *keep* (*shamar*) is sometimes translated as "guard," "safeguard," "take care of," and "look after." *Shamar* indicates a loving, caring, sustaining kind of keeping.

In our worship services, we often conclude with the blessing from Numbers 6:24: "The LORD bless you and keep you. . . ." In the original Hebrew text, the word here for "keep" is *shamar.* When we invoke God's blessing to *keep* us, we are not asking that God would keep us in a kind of preserved, inactive state. Instead, we are calling on God to keep us in all of our vitality, with all our energy and beauty. The keeping we expect of God when we invoke this ancient blessing is one that nurtures all of our life-sustaining and life-fulfilling relationships—with family, neighbors, and friends; with the land, air, and water of the earth; and of course with God.

So too with our keeping of God's creation. Our relationship to creation must be a loving, caring, keeping relationship. When we fulfill God's mandate to *keep* the creation, we make sure that the creatures and other living things under our care are maintained so that they can flourish. They must remain connected with members of the same species, with the many other species with which they interact, and with the soil, air, and water they depend on.

As God *keeps* believing people, so God's people should *keep* his creation.

2 THE FRUITFULNESS PRINCIPLE

We should enjoy but not destroy creation's fruitfulness.

God's blessing of fruitfulness is for the whole creation. In Genesis 1, God declares, "Let the water teem with living creatures, and let birds fly above the earth across the vault of the sky" (1:20). And God blesses these creatures with fruitfulness: "Be fruitful and increase in number and fill the water in the seas, and let the birds increase on the earth" (1:22). God also says, "Let the land produce living creatures according to their kinds, creatures that move along the ground, and wild animals, each according to its kind" (1:24).

God's creation reflects God's fruitful work, giving to land and life what satisfies and sustains it. Psalm 104:10-13 expresses this beautifully:

> He makes springs pour water into the ravines;
>> it flows between the mountains.
> They give water to all the beasts of the field;
>> the wild donkeys quench their thirst.
> The birds of the air nest by the waters;
>> they sing among the branches.
> He waters the mountains from his upper chambers;
>> the land is satisfied by the fruit of his work.

In addition, Psalm 23:2-3 describes how our providing God gives us rest "in green pastures," leads us "beside quiet waters," and "refreshes" our souls.

As God's fruitful work brings fruit to creation, so should ours. As God provides for all his creatures, so should we who are created to reflect God's image. As Noah cared for God's creatures when they were threatened with extinction, so should we. In Noah's time a flood of water covered the land. In our time floods of people in many places sprawl across the land, often displacing God's other creatures, limiting *their* potential to fulfill their blessing and God's command to be fruitful. To those who would allow a human flood across the land at the expense of all other creatures, the prophet Isaiah warns, "Woe to you who add house to house and join field to field till no space is left and you live alone in the land" (Isa. 5:8).

So while we are expected to enjoy creation and its many fruits, we may not destroy the *fruitfulness* that creation's fullness depends on. Like Noah, we must preserve and care for God's many species whose interactions and relationships with each other and with land and water make up the fabric of the biosphere. We must let the profound admonition of Ezekiel 34:18 echo in our minds: "Is it not enough for you to feed on the good pasture? Must you also trample the rest of your pasture with your feet? Is it not enough for you to drink clear water? Must you also muddy the rest with your feet?"

3 THE SABBATH PRINCIPLE

We must provide for creation's sabbath rests.

In Exodus 20 and Deuteronomy 5, God commands us to set aside one day in seven as a day of rest for people and for animals. This sabbath day is given to help us all get "off the treadmill," to protect us all from the hazards of continuous work, to help us pull our lives together again. It's a time to worship the Lord and enjoy the fruits of his creation, a time for rest and restoration. In Exodus 23:12, God commands, "Six days do your work, but on the seventh day do not work, so that your ox and your donkey may rest, and so that the slave born in your household and the foreigner living among you may be refreshed."

The same chapter in Scripture says that the land also must have its time of sabbath rest. Nothing in all creation must be relentlessly pressed. "For six years you are to sow your fields and harvest the crops, but during the seventh year let the land lie unplowed and unused. Then the poor among your people may get food from it, and the wild animals may eat what they leave. Do the same with your vineyard and your olive grove" (23:10-11).

Does this command create a problem for people? Leviticus 25:20-21 says, "You may ask, 'What will we eat in the seventh year if we do not plant or harvest our crops?'" God's answer: "I will send you such a blessing in the sixth year that the land will yield enough for three years." God was instructing people not to worry but to practice his law so that the land would be *fruitful*. "If you follow my decrees and are careful to obey my commands, I will send you rain in its season, and the ground will yield its crops and the trees their fruit" (Lev. 26:3-4).

In the New Testament, Jesus clearly defines for us the meaning of sabbath in our lives: the sabbath is made for those who are served by it—not the other way around (Mark 2:27). The sabbath is made for people and, through them, for all the rest of God's creation. The sabbath year is given to protect the land from relentless exploitation, to help it rejuvenate, to give it a time of rest and restoration.

This sabbath is not merely a legalistic requirement; it's a profound principle. That's why in some farming communities the land is allowed to rest every *second* year, because that is what it needs. The sabbath is made for the land—not the land for the sabbath. The sabbath law is therefore not restricted to agriculture but applies to all of creation. It affects our use of water and air, for example, as we discharge our exhaust, smoke, sewage, and other things we "throw away." God speaks strongly on this issue:

> "If you will not listen to me and carry out all these commands,
> and if you reject my decrees and abhor my laws . . . and so vio-
> late my covenant . . . your land will be laid waste, and your cities
> will lie in ruins. Then the land will enjoy its sabbath years all the
> time it lies desolate . . . then the land will rest and enjoy its sab-
> baths. All the time that it lies desolate, the land will have the rest
> it did not have during the sabbaths you lived in it."
> —*Leviticus 26:14-15, 33-35*

These are harsh words from the holy Creator who is concerned for his creation. But God's promises of blessing are equally powerful for all who will listen:

> "If you keep your feet from breaking the Sabbath and from doing
> as you please . . . then you will find joy in the Lord, and I will
> cause you to ride in triumph on the heights of the land. . . . "
>
> —*Isaiah 58:13-14*

4 THE DISCIPLESHIP PRINCIPLE

We must be disciples of Jesus Christ—the Creator, Sustainer, and Reconciler of all things.

No question about it—the Bible calls us to be disciples, or *followers after* someone. But we are not to be disciples of the first Adam, who neglected to serve (*'abad*) and keep (*shamar*) the creation. We must not follow those who choose to go their own way and do their own thing.

Instead, the Bible tells us, we must be disciples of "the last Adam," Jesus Christ (1 Cor. 15:45). In John 3:16 the New Testament teaches that God loved the world so much that he gave his only Son—to bring true life, to make things right again. "For as in Adam all die, so in Christ all will be made alive" (1 Cor. 15:22).

All who follow Jesus follow the example of the one who makes all things new, the one who makes all things right again (Rev. 21:5). Colossians 1:19-20 puts it this way: "God was pleased to have all his fullness dwell in him, and through him to reconcile to himself *all things*."

Who is this Christ we are to follow? He is the one *in whom* and *for whom* all things were created (Col. 1:16). He is the one *through whom* God made the universe and *through whom* God redeems his people (John 1:3; Col. 1:16, 20; Heb. 1:3).

God reaches out sacrificially to make things right again. Jesus Christ, the final Adam, undoes the damage done by the first Adam and his followers. While Adam's followers bring death and degradation, Christ brings life and restoration (Rom. 5:12-17). The children of God work as followers and disciples of the final Adam. People who are happy being Christ's servant stewards are people for whom the whole creation is eagerly looking (Rom. 8:19).

We must, then, be disciples of Jesus Christ. We walk in the footsteps of the one who reconciles all things. We walk the path of the one who takes the form of a reconciling servant. As disciples of the last Adam, we work to reconcile all things to God in Christ.

5 THE KINGDOM PRIORITY PRINCIPLE

We must seek first the kingdom of God.

Our culture today proclaims, "Seek first a job (money, success), and all other things will be yours as well." It is tempting to yield to this message and to follow people whose highest priority is to gather up immense material gains. But Jesus advises us to seek first the kingdom of God and God's way of doing things; then everything else we need will be given to us as well (Matt. 6:33).

Personal happiness, joy, and fulfillment are not what we seek first of all in life. Instead we seek the kingdom of God and strive to sustain and renew God's creation. In seeking God's kingdom, we discover that happiness and joy are *by-products* of our stewardship; fulfillment comes as a *result* of seeking the kingdom.

Who will inherit this kingdom? Believers who seek it as their first priority. Its inheritance is not for people who arrogantly exploit their neighbors, the land, and earth's creatures for all they are worth. Nor is the inheritance for those who carelessly and knowingly destroy the earth.

Seeking God's kingdom first is our calling, our vocation. We affirm this calling whenever we pray as Jesus taught us: "Our Father in heaven, hallowed be your name, your kingdom come, your will be done *on earth*. . ." (Matt. 6:9-10).

6 THE CONTENTMENT PRINCIPLE

We must seek true contentment.

The fruitful and beautiful creation did not satisfy our first parents and succeeding generations. Even though God promised not to forsake or leave them, people chose to go their own way—grasping more and more from the creation for selfish advancement. In our day we feel the effects of this relentless pressing of land and life to produce more—ever more. This relentless pressing is what is so seriously degrading God's creation today. Everyone's prayer today should be that of Psalm 119:36: "Turn my heart toward your statutes and not toward selfish gain."

If accumulating the goods of creation is selfish gain, then what is godly gain? Godly gain is doing the work God would have us do in the world. In 1 Timothy 6:6 we learn that "godliness with contentment is great gain." Contentment means aiming to have the things that will sustain us while not pressing beyond that. An Amish saying based on this passage goes like this: "To desire to be rich is to desire to have more than what we need to be content."

Why is it important not to pass the point of contentment? In the words of 1 Timothy 6:11, by not passing this point we can "pursue righteousness, godliness, faith, love, endurance and gentleness." Hebrews 13:5 puts it this way: "Keep your lives free from the love of money and be content with what you have, because God has said, 'Never will I leave you; never will I forsake you.'"

Being content helps us personally, and it helps preserve creation's integrity. All the things we use, all the things we make, everything we manipulate, everything we accumulate derives from creation itself. If we learn to seek godly contentment as our great gain, we will take and shape less of God's earth. We will demand less from the land. We will leave room for God's other creatures. We will be responsible stewards, caretakers, keepers of creation. We will regularly allow creation to heal itself and perpetuate its fruitfulness, to the glory and praise of its Maker.

7 THE PRAXIS PRINCIPLE

We must practice what we believe.

The Scriptures admonish us to act on what we know is right. Merely knowing God's requirements for stewardship is not enough. Merely believing in God is not enough, for Scripture tells us that even demons believe in God (James 2:19). We must practice God's requirements, or they do no good.

The failure of God's people to act on what they know is right is well-documented—and challenged—in the pages of Scripture:

> "My people come to you, as they usually do, and sit before you
> to hear your words, but they do not put them into practice. Their
> mouths speak of love, but their hearts are greedy for unjust gain.
> Indeed, to them you are nothing more than one who sings love
> songs with a beautiful voice and plays an instrument well, for
> they hear your words, but they do not put them into practice."
> —*Ezekiel 33:31-32*

> "Why do you call me, 'Lord, Lord,' and do not do what I say?"
> —*Luke 6:46*

Christian environmental stewardship does not end with the last chapter of a book on the topic. Instead, studying the Bible to learn God's requirements for creation care marks a beginning point. It brings us directly to the question *Now what must we do?* The challenge before us now is to move forward and put what we know and believe into practice.

8 THE CON-SERVANCY PRINCIPLE

We must return creation's service to us with service of our own.

This principle overarches all the others. The word *conservancy*, as you may know, refers to conservation and often denotes an organization that regulates fisheries and/or protects other natural resources. In this discussion I hyphenate this word to draw attention to its root meaning—*con* + *serve* means "to serve with."

You remember that, as we considered the earthkeeping principle, we noted from Genesis 2:15 that Adam was expected to *serve* the creation and to *keep* it. The Hebrew word *'abad* ("serve") in this passage occurs 290 times in the Old Testament, and it is most often translated as "serve," as in Joshua 24:15: "Choose for yourselves this day whom you will serve. . . . As for me and my household, we will serve the LORD."

The various Bible translations of *'abad* in Genesis 2:15—"serve," "till," "dress," and "work"—relate to worthy service. God calls us to give the garden of creation our caring service.

We already know from experience with the "beautiful book" of creation that this garden serves us. It serves us with good food, beauty, herbs, fiber, medicine, pleasant microclimates, continual soil-making, nutrient processing, and seed production. The garden and the larger biosphere provide what ecologists call "ecosystem services" such as water purification by evaporation and percolation, moderation of flood peaks and drought flows by river-system wetlands, development of soils from the weathering of rocks, and moderation of local climates by nearby bodies of water. Yet Genesis addresses *our* service to the garden. The garden's service *to us* is implicit; service *from us* to the garden is explicit.

Like Adam, we are expected to return the service of the garden with service of our own. This is a reciprocal service, a "service with"—in other words, a *con-service*, a *con-servancy*, a *con-servation*. This reciprocal service defines an engaging relationship between garden and gardener, between the biosphere and its safeguarding stewards.

So we can call this "never taking from creation without returning service of our own" the *Con-Servancy Principle* (or *Con-Servation Principle*). Our love of our Creator God, God's love of the creation, and our imaging this love of God—all join together to commission us as *con-servers* of creation. As *con-servers*, we follow the example of the second Adam—Jesus Christ (see 1 Cor. 15:22, 45).

Suggestions for Group Session

GETTING STARTED

We don't usually think of the Bible as a kind of handbook on how to care for God's creation. But in part that's what it is. The Bible has much to teach us about right living in relationship to God, to other people, and to all of creation. We know that the Bible's teaching is done in the context of knowing and celebrating God as Creator and Sustainer of all things. So we really can expect the Bible to inform us on right living in God's creation—and so it does. In this chapter we open ourselves and our minds to the Bible's teachings on caring for the earth we are entrusted with—on "serving with" the earth to honor and praise the Lord, our Maker and Savior.

Scripture Readings
Genesis 1:26-28; 2:15
John 1:1-5; 3:16-21
Colossians 1:15-20
Revelation 11:15-18

Opening Prayer
Begin by thanking God for the beauty of creation, for the testimony it gives of God's everlasting power and divinity, and for the testimony of God in the Bible. Express together your appreciation for God's not leaving us without guidance. As

you praise God for showing his love and care for creation, pray also that we—imaging God—may also love and care for creation. Pray that in our world today we may take very seriously the teachings of Scripture, specifically noting biblical teachings on earthkeeping, fruitfulness, and sabbath.

FOR DISCUSSION

What are some good texts for framing?

1. Suppose that you were asked to select three passages from the Bible about caring for creation to be reproduced on wall plaques. Which ones would you choose?

Are biblical teachings about creation relevant today?

2. Write out the passage from Ezekiel 34:18 about the muddying of water and the trampling of pasture land.
   - Is this passage relevant to the degradation of water and land today? Explain.
   - Does this passage tell us anything about how we should treat the rest of creation? Why or why not?

3. What does Isaiah 5:8 say to us about the way we use land today?

4. What are some ways we can provide for creation's "sabbath rest"? (See Ex. 23:10-11.)

5. Share your thoughts on the relationship between Genesis 1:26-28 and Genesis 2:15. How do these two passages help to explain each other? What do they tell us about our relationship to God and our relationship to God's creation?

What's your stewardship rating?

6. On a scale of 1 (poor) to 10 (excellent), how would you rate your personal stewardship of God's creation? Share your rating and the reasons for it with others in the group, and discuss ways in which you could help each other as you strive to do God's will in caring for creation.

CLOSING

The Bible is a rich source of wisdom, and its depth becomes more and more evident as we "turn it about," thinking deeply about what it has to teach us.

As you close this session, thank God together for the Bible, its depth of meaning, and for what it brings to our lives as we work to live in obedience and love for our Lord. Pray specifically for the Spirit's encouragement and empowerment to act on what you've learned here about earthkeeping, fruitfulness, sabbath rest for creation, and serving with the creation to honor God. Then conclude by reading in unison the ancient blessing found in Numbers 6:24-26.

May the Lord bless and *keep* you!

Note: The next session requires a slow, reflective reading. You'll want to set aside extra time to thoughtfully consider what it says as it lays out a theological foundation for understanding how we should serve as individuals and as the church in and with God's creation.

FOUR

A Theological Perspective on Creation Care

The biblical principles of *Con-Servancy, Earthkeeping, Fruitfulness, Sabbath, Discipleship, Kingdom Priority, Contentment*, and *Praxis* lie at the heart of creation care, or Christian environmental stewardship. They also lie at the heart of gardening. It is, after all, in a garden—the Garden of Eden—that the Bible introduces us to responsible care for creation. So it is fruitful for us to begin this chapter by focusing on gardens and gardening as we work to discover more fully the meaning of stewardship. It also is fitting to begin where we left off in the previous chapter—with the Con-Servancy Principle.

We learn from the text from which the Con-Servancy Principle comes (Gen. 2:15) that Adam and Eve were expected to return the service of the garden with service of their own. God intends this *relationship* between gardeners and garden so that all might flourish and be fruitful. This relationship of reciprocal service is vital to responsive gardening and is the key to garden stewardship. This back-and-forth sustaining relationship is the same kind of service that engages us with the biosphere—the great symphony of life that envelops our earth. And, wonderfully, what we discover from our relationship with the garden and the biosphere is that they have a lot to teach us!

The garden, with its many leafy and floral species, with its colorful and life-perpetuating fruitfulness, helps us see how we gain knowledge by "reading" the things God has made, and how we expand on this knowledge by learning from others who delight in gardening—from neighbors and relatives, master gardeners, field naturalists, ecologists, climatologists, soil scientists, and other amateurs and professionals. They too gain their knowledge by reading the creation and by reading things from others who also read creation's "beautiful book." Their delight brings them to study things great and small, and their learning comes to us in the form of lectures, gardening manuals, field guides, recordings, magazines, books, videos, and television specials—not to mention refereed papers that receive careful scrutiny and affirmation by full-time students of creation.

GARDENERS AND STEWARDS

As we think about gardening and stewardship, a simple way to begin is to think about caring for a "house plant" in a flower pot. By our "back-and-forth" relationship with it, we soon learn what our plant needs to survive and flourish. As we shift its location and give it nutrients and water, it teaches us its needs—for fertile soil, sunlight, water, temperature, and more. It responds to our care with growth and color and beauty—a song of praise to its Creator. When light is available, the plant also produces some of the oxygen we need (by way of photosynthesis) in return for using some of the carbon dioxide we expire—a valuable provision from our Creator.

Moving to our garden outside, we find that it teaches us more. We learn how we can bring ourselves to provide for the needs of individual species and the garden as a whole. As gardeners, we are shaped and encouraged to grow as caretakers in accord with what the garden needs to flourish and be fruitful. We serve the garden's needs and enjoyment, even as it serves ours.

Being stewards of God's wider creation—the biosphere—is much like that. We learn directly about the biosphere by our own observations and study, and we learn indirectly from others. We learn what is needed to bring ourselves into harmony with the requirements for sustaining the biosphere. The essence of creation stewardship involves adapting to and acting in accord with creation's needs to sustain itself and to flourish with abundant life. In return, creation provides the habitat for us in which we also can enjoy flourishing, abundant life.

As we learn from the biosphere, our delight increases. More than that, our awareness and respect for it and its creatures also increases. As we learn more, we are inspired to live in harmony with creation and to learn even more. And when the biosphere and its supportive provisions for us and other life are threatened, we work to safeguard its flourishing and abundant life.

Pause at this point to reread the epigraph at the beginning of this book, written in 1554 by John Calvin. Then read it again, exploring your thoughts that come to mind in light of our "back-and-forth" relationship with God's creation. Is it remarkable that Calvin could express these thoughts hundreds of years ago? Why or why not?

Now, just as there are great differences between a flower in a pot and the many interactive species in a garden, there are great differences between a garden and the entire creation! One truly amazing difference is that there are vast parts of creation that need no help from us. We don't have to draw up water to form the clouds, produce the thunder and lightning of great storms, give orders to the morning, or govern earth's climate system. Neither do we have to guide and arrange the constellations of the heavens, cause the eagle to soar, construct a fully functioning hippopotamus, or call forth earth's vegetation to cover a new lava field. Nor do we have to direct earth's living creatures to live in harmony with their habitats, find food, reproduce, and otherwise flourish. God provides for and takes care of all these things—and much more!

So we are not gardeners of the entire creation. We are not even gardeners of the biosphere. But we are its stewards! At the very least we are stewards of everything in the biosphere on which our human life and society have an impact. And since our impact today has become global, it is increasingly necessary to know that we are stewards of the entire earth. This also makes it necessary for us to explore together what our stewardship of the biosphere means—practically, ethically, and theologically.

BAG OF RESOURCES? OR BEAUTIFUL BOOK?

From the Scriptures we know that ever since the creation of human beings, God has been in an interactive *relationship* with us. Ever since God breathed into us the breath of life, making us in his image, God has been with us, and we have belonged to our Maker. More than that, God made us his imagebearers so that we might reflect his love and care for the world and thus bring glory and honor to him. People have often affirmed and celebrated this relationship—in which the Lord promises to be our God and we promise to honor God as his people. The covenant of circumcision was one of the earliest examples of this mutual relationship (see Gen. 17:1-8). Then about two thousand years later the sign and seal of baptism affirmed this relationship for New Testament believers in Christ, who fulfilled all the requirements of the earlier covenant, reconciling us with God, opening the way for us to be saved from sin so that we may live with God forever.

History shows all too clearly, however, that we have broken our promises to God again and again. Early on, when humankind was young, we pressed beyond the boundaries of the garden God gave us. As a result, we came to know (to experience) evil as well as good (Gen. 2:16-17; 3:11). And this pressing has continued through the millennia so that creation's testimony to God's glory, divinity, and eternal power is now often obscured (see Ps. 19:1; Rom. 1:18-23). Our pressing has gone so far that we have even come to look on creation as a kind of "bag of resources." This stands in contrast to thinking of God's creation as a "beautiful book," as we have noted in earlier chapters. Moreover, the wonder of God's provisions—for example, everyday photosynthesis—is now mainly taken for granted.

Worse yet, God's provisions are now often regarded as mere mechanisms, which we sometimes even think we can improve. In many ways this kind of thinking and acting has overtaken us and brought the whole creation into a kind of suffering and groaning (Rom. 8:20-21).

As I think of the "beautiful book" metaphor, I am reminded of a great library. We can think of the Library of Congress, for example, or one of our great university libraries, as a great treasure house of recorded learning and knowledge. Imagine, though, that we come upon a library without understanding or caring about reading its texts. Imagine that we might not even know that the printed characters in its books make up words and sentences. Suppose also that—not recognizing these as stores of knowledge—we view these books as fuel, nicely packaged and arranged in neat stacks for us to use in our wood-burning stoves! (Author and scholar Thomas Cahill tells us in his book *How the Irish Saved Civilization* that people in ages past have actually viewed books this way.)

This illustration hits home for me in the great marsh just outside my back door. This peatland on which I live is itself a history book. Beneath its surface are preserved, layer by layer, yearly records of its own history. Each of its annually deposited layers contains pollen grains that fell from wetland plants or blew in from surrounding hillsides. The layers also contain seeds and snail shells left from the life that once flourished there. Remarkably, some of these layers also contain volcanic ash. Whenever great volcanic eruptions in the distant past gave off ash that blew around the globe, some of it dropped into my peatland. The content and amount of this ash is different between layers that mark various centuries.

I have learned to read this ash and pollen. And from pollen, for example, I learn that in its early years my marsh was surrounded by a spruce and fir forest; then later it became part of an open prairie in what is now southern Wisconsin. From the volcanic ash I learn something about the timing and intensity of the blowup of Mount Mazama—the eruption that created Crater Lake in southwestern Oregon. Winds from the western coast of North America carried its ash along and deposited it here before the time of Jesus Christ.

Yet, remarkable and unique as creation's great history books are as sources of knowledge, large tracts of their "sodden pages," entire volumes, and whole libraries are being destroyed. Some peat volumes are dried and burned in stoves to heat homes on Irish moors, some are ground up to provide sphagnum mulch for gardens, and some are drained and left to be decomposed into water and carbon dioxide by their exposure to atmospheric oxygen. In a sense, then, we really do burn up and ruin storehouses of valuable knowledge today—not because we do not appreciate information and knowledge, but because we do not appreciate or even recognize the language in which some of these volumes are written.

Thanks to the work of leaders in conservation efforts, however—perhaps most notably a hundred years ago in North America by the U.S. president Theodore Roosevelt—there are hundreds of preserves on our continent today in the form of national forests, bird sanctuaries, protected wetlands, and national parks. These efforts have also been modeled around the world to safeguard pages and chapters of the "beautiful book" of creation.

STEWARDSHIP IN OUR DIFFERENT PLACES

As we appreciate creation and read and learn from the pages of this elegant book, we do so in the places we live—across the continent and around the globe. Our places of living and doing include countrysides, towns, villages, and cities. The regions we live in feature all kinds of ecosystems, including tropical forests, boreal forests, prairies and steppes, mountains, deserts, wetlands, oceans, and more. Our stewardship is defined and shaped by the places we live and by our local ecosystems. And whatever our stewardship is locally, it will join with a regional and global stewardship, informed by other stewards around the globe.

What this means is that our stewardship is rich and full. Our stewardship of the biosphere is not only far-ranging but also dynamic. It is dynamic because it is continually informed by the consequences of our and others' actions in the world. In our various regions of the world we will not always be doing the same kinds of stewardly activities, but in our responses to what we learn from creation we will often change what we do—all in the direction of sustaining the integrity of creation.

What does stewardship of creation accomplish in our world today? Here's a definition that helps answer this question: *Stewardship of creation dynamically shapes and reshapes human behavior to sustain God's creation. Stewardship of creation works to do this for the particular places we live, for the ecosystems of which our places are a part, and for the biosphere.*

GOD IN RELATIONSHIP WITH US AND CREATION

Stewardship of all God's gifts and blessings has been God's expectation of people throughout history. And this expectation comes not as a dictate from a distant deity, but from God *in relationship* with us. We are people created in God's image to relate in communion with our Maker and Provider. Beginning with God's communion with Adam and Eve in the garden and on through the great dramatic history of redemption, God remains in *relationship*—both with us and with creation. This relationship continues also into the future. God's immanence—"God with us" (Matt. 1:23)—sustains this relationship. God's transcendence—God as sovereign and eternal—assures us that the whole universe is in God's hands. This is true from before the beginning of time, and it is true forever into the future. God's immanence and transcendence provide the awesome context of the three-way relationship among God, creation, and human beings.

All of this assures us that we are not mere afterthoughts of God in creation. As imagers of God's love, we are created to care for and serve creation, including other human creatures, on behalf of God. Creation stewardship calls for imaging

God's care and keeping for all that the Lord has made. As images we do God's will; as imagers we reflect God's glory.

Our *relationship* began when God breathed into us the breath of life and we became living beings (Gen. 2:7). And when God gave us the vocation of serving and safeguarding the garden (2:15), we entered a three-way relationship that provides a framework for our life and living on earth, the framework for stewardship.

IS CREATION A LOST CAUSE?

Many people today—both "people of faith" and others—are wondering if creation, in all its degradations and lost treasures, has become a lost cause. So many things are damaged or broken in the biosphere that we might wonder, "How can any of this possibly be repaired?" Having learned about the degradations human beings have brought about in creation, some might advocate that we "just give up!" Lest we lean toward that kind of thinking or develop some perverse extension of it, like "Eat, drink, and be merry, for tomorrow we die!"—or perhaps something even worse—we may need to come to grips with our responsibility to serve God and his creation. For most of us in North America, this may mean we need to serve more responsibly than we or our ancestors have done. It is important to hear what Scripture says about our responsibility. And while statements like the following can be quite sobering, especially in view of God's final judgment, they can help us get back on track if we have strayed. Revelation 11:18, for example, states that "the time [will] come for judging the dead, and for rewarding . . . people who revere [God's] name, both great and small—and for destroying those who destroy the earth."

Of course, it is not only this declaration that affirms God's continuing *relationship* with us and with creation. This statement is backed up and preceded by many words of promise and blessing, including what we call "signs and seals." All of this assures us that God does not abandon the creation. And neither does God abandon us!

SIGNS AND SEALS

In the divine order of things, our *relationship* with God, including the promises God has made to us, is confirmed with signs and seals—and these have a lot to do with creation stewardship. One of the oldest signs in creation that reminds us of God's care, for example, is the rainbow. After God sent a great flood to destroy most of humanity for its wickedness, the Lord made promises to Noah and his family, who with all kinds of animals were saved from the flood—declaring that the rainbow would be a sign that God would never again send such a flood "to destroy all life" (Gen. 9:15).

Baptism is another example. Baptism is a sign and seal of being bonded to Christ. It also testifies that as surely as we can use water to wash our bodies clean, we can trust through faith in Christ that the Spirit of Christ washes away our sins (Heidelberg Catechism, Q&A 73).

Still another example is the bread and wine (or juice) in the sacrament of the Lord's Supper (Holy Communion, Eucharist). The bread and wine are signs and seals that confirm the benefits gained for us by the death and resurrection of Jesus:

> First,
>> as surely as I see with my eyes
>>> the bread of the Lord broken for me
>>> and the cup given to me,
>> so surely
>>> his body was offered and broken for me
>>> and his blood poured out for me on the cross.
> Second,
>> as surely as
>>> I receive from the hand of the one who serves,
>>> and taste with my mouth
>>>> the bread and cup of the Lord,
>>>> given me as sure signs of Christ's body and blood,
>> so surely
>>> he nourishes and refreshes my soul for eternal life
>> with his crucified body and poured-out blood.
>
> *—Heidelberg Catechism, Q&A 75*

God uses the "stuff" of creation, material things, to seal his saving promises to us.

SON OF GOD, SON OF MAN

Creation is not a lost cause. God has confirmed this fact by the birth, life, ministry, death, and resurrection of Jesus Christ, the Word who "became flesh" for our sake and "made his dwelling among us" (John 1:14). The Son of God, who is fully God, was with the Creator "in the beginning," and is the one through whom "all things were made" (1:2-3). The Son has himself entered God's own creation to redeem it and us from the destruction we began when we first sinned against God (Gen. 3). God sent Jesus because he "so loved the world" and "everything in it" (Ps. 24:1; John 3:16).

As the *Logos* (the Word) through whom all things were created, Jesus Christ became the key to interpreting the history of the world and the meaning of life. Back in the time when the apostle John wrote his gospel account of the life and ministry of Christ, Greek philosophers commonly used the word *logos* to refer to the unifying force of the universe. In light of the statements John makes about Jesus—"Through him all things were made" and "In him was life" (John 1:3-4)—we can see that John was using *logos* to speak of Jesus as the divine Word who holds all things together (see also Col. 1:15-20). By undoing the degrading works of the first Adam and his followers, and by leading us in doing what the first Adam was supposed to do, Jesus is reconciling all things to God (see Rom. 5:8-11; 2 Cor. 5:17-20; Col. 1:20).

Jesus Christ, the Word incarnate, expressing God's profound love for the world (John 3:16-17), moves into creation to break the chains of sin and its oppressing, degrading effects on creation. Jesus Christ renews the life of the earth. Jesus is the hope of the world, and we, his followers, are his ambassadors (2 Cor. 5:20), representing him as witnesses before all people and as stewards of creation.

All the principles on creation care that we have gleaned from Scripture originate, reverberate, and find their fulfillment in Jesus Christ—the *Logos* through whom the whole creation has its meaning and destiny. Adopting the mind of Christ, we take on his humility, not counting ourselves as divine but as servants (Phil. 2:6-8). Filled with the Spirit of God to become like the second Adam (2 Cor. 3:18) rather than the first Adam, we become servants of the garden, of humanity, of the whole creation—to the glory of God.

Christians often speak of their ultimate destination as "heaven." The Bible speaks of heaven as the "dwelling place" of God. Yet it's a mistake to think of heaven as a place, like some far-off planet or galaxy. In the biblical sense, heaven is that spiritual dimension of reality which we now cannot see, but which is as real as the material creation. As the Nicene Creed says, "We believe in one God, the Father almighty, maker of heaven and earth, of all things visible and invisible."

God's plan of salvation is not to transport us to some disembodied spiritual place, but to restore and renew the creation. In the end, according to Revelation 21, there will be "a new heaven and a new earth" (see also Isa. 65:17). God's saving purpose does not ignore the creation or leave it behind in a gigantic conflagration—but renews it. Our very physical bodies are to be resurrected, though the exact form they will take eludes our understanding (and Paul's—see 1 Cor. 15). The pioneer and guarantor of that physical future is Jesus Christ, who rose *bodily* from the dead, "the firstfruits" of those who believe. He ascended *bodily* into heaven to rule over all things, and one day he will return bodily and physically to the earth.

Christians need to reclaim the stewardship of this creation in the light of the sheer physicality of salvation in the new creation.

Suggestions for Group Session

GETTING STARTED

We got under way in chapter 3 by exploring biblical teachings about creation care. We found numerous Scripture texts that are very useful for learning God's will for us in creation. In the chapter for this session we build on that work to explore things more deeply and theologically. We relate Scripture to Scripture, reflecting on the meaning of the Bible's identification of Christ as the second Adam and the

Word Incarnate, pondering even the signs and seals of God's promises in relation to the work of Jesus Christ.

Scripture Readings

    Genesis 2:7, 15; 9:12-17; 11:3-4; 17:7
    Psalm 19:1
    John 1:1-4, 14; 3:16-17
    Romans 1:20-23; 8:19-22
    1 Corinthians 15:22
    2 Corinthians 3:18; 5:17-20
    Colossians 1:15-20
    Revelation 11:18

Opening Prayer

We can thank God for the great depth of the Scriptures and for the richness that Scripture study brings to our understanding of God's will for our lives and for creation. We can also give thanks for God's gift of the second Adam, Jesus Christ, and we can pray that increasingly we might discover what it means to follow the one who upholds and reconciles all things.

FOR DISCUSSION

What do we confess, and why?

1.   A theological statement of faith on the topic of our study is provided in *Our World Belongs to God: A Contemporary Testimony.* Excerpts from this testimony follow (st. 10, 14, 16, 18-19, 24-26, 28-29). Reflect and share your thoughts on how these statements based on Scripture can help us share with others our role as stewards of the creation ruled and held together by Christ as King today.

     10. As God's creatures we are made in his image
         to represent him on earth
         and to live in loving communion with him.
         By sovereign appointment we are
         earthkeepers and caretakers:
         loving our neighbor,
         tending the creation,
         and meeting our needs.
         God uses our skills
         in the unfolding and well-being of his world.

     14. Early in human history
         our first parents . . . fell for Satan's lie
         and sinned!

61

They forgot their place;
they tried to be like God.
But as sinners they feared
the nearness of God
and hid from him.

16. When humans no longer show God's image,
all creation suffers.
We abuse the creation or idolize it.
We are estranged from our Creator,
from our neighbor, and from all that God has made.

18. In all our strivings
to excuse
or save ourselves,
we stand condemned
before the God of Truth.
But our world,
broken and scarred,
still belongs to God.
He holds it together
and gives us hope.

19. While justly angry
God did not turn his back
on a world bent on destruction;
he turned his face to it in love.
With patience and tender care he set out
on the long road of redemption
to reclaim the lost as his people
and the world as his kingdom.

24. God remembered his promise
to reconcile the world to himself;
he has come among us
in Jesus Christ,
the eternal Word made flesh.
He is the long-awaited Savior,
fully human and fully divine,
conceived by the Spirit of God
and born of the virgin Mary.

25. In the events of his earthly life —
his temptations and suffering,

his teaching and miracles,
his battles with demons and talks with sinners—
Jesus made present in deed and in word
the coming rule of God.

26. As the second Adam he chose
the path we had rejected.
As our representative,
serving God perfectly,
and loving even those who scorned him,
Christ showed us how
a righteous child of God lives.

28. Being both God and man,
Jesus is the only Mediator
between God and his people.
He alone paid the debt of our sin;
there is no other Savior! . . .

29. Jesus ascended in triumph
to his heavenly throne.
There he hears our prayers,
pleads our cause before the Father,
and rules the world.
Blessed are all
who take refuge in him.

Of whom are we disciples today?
2. With other group members, make a list of actions you might take regarding creation if you were a follower of the first Adam. Then make a contrasting list of actions you can take as a disciple of the second Adam. Which of the actions in the second list are things you already do? Which ones could you easily begin doing, if you put your mind to it, in Christ? Which ones will take a lot of effort, perhaps together with lots of other people? Explain.

What is our motive for creation care?
3. Discuss the difference between the following motivations for creation care and keeping: gratitude, obedience, love, guilt. What difference does our motivation for creation care make?

Are endangered species worth our time and money?

4. A student I knew, after coming back from observing the Kirtland's warbler—an endangered species of bird that nests only in a small area of jack pines near Mio, Michigan—was asked what she thought about the efforts of conservation workers to protect and keep this species. The student replied, "That's an awful lot of money to spend on a silly little bird." In response, her questioner replied, "Yes, the price of gopher wood is very high these days!" (gopher wood being the material from which Noah built the ark). What's the connection? Discuss the issues this comment raises, and substantiate your arguments biblically.

How important is the concept of sabbath keeping in connection with creation?

5. Leviticus 25 talks about giving the land a sabbath rest every year. A farmer friend of mine in Neerlandia, Alberta, lets the land rest every second year. He maintains that this is what his land needs. What do you think of my friend's application of Scripture here? In what other ways can we apply the concept of sabbaths to our care for creation?

What does it mean to image God's care of creation?

6. How would you describe God's care for creation, and how can we image that care in the places and regions where we live? How can we contribute to global creation care?

Is creation care really important for Christians?

7. Is a polluted world and the loss of species a concern for Christians? Is it a concern for your church's evangelism committee or outreach efforts? Should it be? Why or why not?

CLOSING

As you close in prayer, express gratitude for the richness of God's revelation in creation and in the Bible, as well as for the minds God has given us, in Christ, to assimilate biblical truth and put it into practice. Pray also that God will prepare each of you, for your next meeting together as well as for each day, to put your knowledge of his will into practice.

Note: The next chapter introduces a mini-workshop you can use for putting creation care into practice in your daily living in ways that can involve your church, household, and larger community. Group leaders especially will want to plan ahead for conducting this workshop during the next group session. (See also an optional procedure under "Suggestions for Group Session" at the end of chapter 5.)

FIVE

Putting Creation Care into Practice

(A Workshop Session)

W hat can we do in our church, household, and larger community to respond to environmental concerns? Once we have looked at this question in the light of biblical teaching, we should not sit passively and watch as God's creation continues to be degraded. We need to put our beliefs into practice. Care for God's creation is not only possible; it is vitally necessary in our time. Honoring God as Creator and imaging God's care for creation, we have an important contribution to make toward right living in our world today.

As we proceed, we need to answer some important questions:

- How do we bring together and present what we have learned so that our church, household, and larger community can catch the vision of caring for creation?
- With the vision in place, how can we put what we know into practice?
- How can we sustain the vision so that we don't lose sight of it when other issues come up in our church, community, and household life?

This chapter helps to address these questions, but not by providing a simple prescription. Rather, this chapter offers a technique for mining ideas from the minds of fellow believers—children and adults, clergy and laypeople, male and female, rich and poor, teacher and student, urbanite and farmer—and putting those ideas together so that Christians and their surrounding communities can increasingly become part of the solution to environmental care in the growing crisis we are facing today.

As we become more aware of God's creation and how it is being degraded, we can identify our churches, homes, and communities as "Creation Care Centers." We can seek to demonstrate our responsibility and privilege in being good stewards of creation. Though we might be guided by the examples of others, each group will also want to develop plans to meet the needs of their local situation while also contributing to assessment and action on regional and global needs. To help you get started, this chapter presents a procedure in the form of a mini-workshop that can be used effectively. (See also an optional procedure described in "Suggestions for Group Session" at the end of this chapter.)

A Mini-Workshop

The procedure described on the following pages will help you generate lots of ideas for making your church, household, or larger community a Creation Care Center. It then guides you to choose the best ideas to put into action.

This procedure enables people to bypass initial roadblocking debates about the validity of ideas or budget and time constraints. It also helps bring specific ideas into an organized, coherent statement to present to church or community leaders who have the authority to move ahead with an action plan. The group or community therefore benefits from the undiluted strengths, talents, and abilities of everyone involved.

The procedure works best with a group of five to fifty people who already share a concern for and an understanding of the various degradations of creation. A one-hour session usually is sufficient to identify and screen ideas. Following the session, results should be summarized and gathered into a document for further development and implementation by your group, church, or community leaders.

Because this process begins with particular local issues and uses available local talent, each resulting Creation Care Center will have its own personality, identity, and character.

PROCEDURE
A. General Setting and Room Arrangement
Set up the room with all chairs in a single circle. Once people are seated, remove extra chairs so that no empty ones remain (but keep extra chairs handy for any latecomers). Bring a supply of index cards or similar-sized sheets of recycled paper. You'll need three cards for each person in the group. Have pencils or pens available for any members who come without them.

B. *Generating Initial Ideas*

When the group is seated, explain that a Creation Care Center is a community, large or small, that intends to honor God as Creator and Sustainer in every way. This mini-workshop aims to help people discover how best to accomplish this goal in the community and region in which they live.

To begin, give two blank cards to each person, noting that people should write on one side only. Then ask, "What specific idea can you think of to make our church (or household or larger community) a Creation Care Center?"

Have people reflect for a few moments and then write their idea on one of the cards. Help group members to think broadly and deeply by asking some additional questions while they are reflecting:

- What is our situation here?
- What local environmental problems need to be addressed?
- How can we become a kind of "window on creation care"—a model of how to care for God's earth?
- What do we have going for us that other congregations (households, communities) do not?
- What special contributions could we make toward the care and keeping of creation?

The purpose of asking these questions at various points while people are reflecting is to help them think creatively. This process can help to free people from real or imagined constraints of having too little money, already full schedules, or the need to "be practical." It encourages them to come up with their best ideas.

When participants have finished writing (after 3 to 5 minutes), ask them to think of another best idea and to write that on the other card. Again ask questions to help people think creatively. Urge them to move beyond the obvious.

C. *"Idea Skimming"*

After group members have finished recording their ideas, have them pass both cards to the person on their right. Repeat this step so that the cards have been passed twice. Then have everyone read both cards carefully. Tell them that when you say "Pass," they should pass the card with the better idea to the person on their right. If both ideas have equal merit, they should select either one to pass.

Again give the signal to pass a card—the better of the two that each person is holding. Repeat this process from three to seven times, but not so often that people might receive a card they had earlier. Explain that this process sifts out best ideas by using a screen of different perspectives. The best ideas will naturally endure the screening of different viewpoints.

When you've decided as a group that you're done passing cards, each person should read aloud the better of the two ideas in his or her hand. Without making comments on the ideas, say "thank you" as you collect each card that is read.

Continue around the circle until each person has read one idea. Stack together the "better idea" cards, and set them aside.

D. More Ideas

Pass out another blank card to each group member. (Each person will now have a blank card and the card with the poorer idea from the previous round.) Now ask everyone to take into account all the ideas they read as they passed cards around earlier. They should also reflect for a minute or two on additional ideas they could write down. Here are some additional idea categories you could mention:

- use of liturgy, sermon, songs, order of worship
- building, grounds, parks, streets
- region, state, nation, world
- animals, plants, woods, fields, wetlands
- earth's energy exchange, soil and land degradation, ecosystem dysfunction, habitat destruction, species extinctions, global toxification, human and cultural abuse

Again ask questions to encourage creative thinking while everyone is reflecting. When everyone has written an idea on a blank card, repeat the passing procedure from three to seven times and conclude with the reading of the better ideas. Again collect each card after it is read, making a second pack to set aside.

E. Filling Remaining Gaps

Ask if any of the remaining cards has a good idea that has not yet been read. If so, group members should read such cards and hand them to you so that you can make a third pack.

At this point you will probably be ready to end this session, having completed the groundwork of your mini-workshop. See suggestions at the end of this chapter for a Bible study activity (if you have time) and for closing today's session.

F. Preparing Results

Together as a group (or having two or three persons assigned to this task), prepare a document based on the contents of the card packs. Identify major topics and sort the cards into those categories. Typical categories that may emerge are Creation Care Committee, other congregational committees, administration, liturgy and worship, building and grounds, community, and so on. Arrange the categories in a logical order, with those that address the administration of your Creation Care Center at the top. Type up the ideas, organized by categories, suggest action plans for implementing the ideas, and add a descriptive title to the document.

G. Distribution of the Results and Follow-Up

After obtaining necessary approvals, distribute the document to all who should receive it. For example, you may consider printing the results in your church newsletter, if that applies. Follow this by examining each identified category and bringing the content of each category to the attention of leaders, committees, or task forces who can follow up on your findings with concrete actions. Use the document together as you take steps to become a Creation Care Center.

IDEAS GLEANED FROM CONGREGATIONS

Stop! The following list of ideas should not be consulted until after group members have generated their own ideas. For additional helpful ideas in your ongoing work as a Creation Care Center, you may wish to consult this list, compiled from several congregations who implemented the preceding mini-workshop.

A. *Creation Care Committee*

1. Form a committee of interested people to advise the church to raise creation awareness, build an understanding of God as Creator, and assist people to become better stewards of our Lord's creation.
2. Publish information on Christian environmental stewardship in your newsletter.
3. Include a selection of books and materials on Christian environmental stewardship in your library, including those with biblical principles, practical suggestions for action, and local natural history and ecology.
4. Provide creation-focused materials for homebound members and residents of nursing homes, including audiotapes of birds, running waters, and weather; provide bird feeders for people's windows, and set up a schedule for keeping the feeders filled.

B. *Worship and Liturgy*

1. Designate one Sunday each season for recognizing our commitment to God's earth.
2. Request a sermon on creation care and keeping.
3. Devote a portion of each worship service to creation awareness and care. (For example, have at least one family report on something they are doing to help take care of God's creation.)
4. Encourage leaders and members to extend the principle of compassion to all living things (human beings, flora, fauna, and the biosphere).
5. Hold a well-planned outdoor worship service on environmental stewardship in a park or in an awe-inspiring creation setting, followed by a picnic.
6. Plan a multigenerational half-day or even two-hour field trip to regain appreciation and concern for God's creation. Include such things as star viewing and delighting in the life of a river.
7. Plant a new church that emphasizes general (natural) revelation—that is, learning from the "beautiful book" of God's creation as well as from the Bible (special revelation). Its mission statement could direct that all members prac-

tice creation stewardship and promote and honor the Lord of creation in all respects.

8. Emphasize how each person can give others an impression of creation awareness and creation care in their everyday work and living.

C. *Building and Grounds*

1. Use a church sign that emphasizes the importance of caring for creation.
2. Have an energy audit to find out ways in which your church and other buildings could use energy more efficiently. Become an "Energy Star Congregation" (Google this term on the Internet).
3. Use energy-efficient lighting and switches that turn off automatically when people are not present and when window light is adequate.
4. Assign someone the responsibility to see that all lights, fans, and air conditioning are turned off when the building is empty.
5. Remodel to save energy, doing such things as insulating, adding solar units, putting in a heat-pump water heater, and installing dropped ceilings where appropriate.
6. Research and develop ways to generate your own electricity (using wind, solar, geothermal, or other energy) and perhaps send surpluses back into the power grid.
7. Set up recycling bins for sorting metal, glass, plastics, paper, and so on. Post signs to remind people of the church's recycling program.
8. Hang appropriate banners and wall-hangings in the halls and meeting area to help raise people's awareness of creation.
9. Make provisions that encourage people to appreciate creation: windows that open, clear glass panes in appropriate locations for viewing creation's beauty, trees and flowers planted at points where they can be seen from inside the building.
10. Develop a naturally self-sustaining park (garden) where people of the community can come to enjoy peace, quiet, plants, trees, animals, and the Lord. Have a sign that states the purpose of the park. Plant berry bushes, trees, and flowers that will attract birds and other animals.
11. Add an open-air covered picnic area to your grounds.
12. Add a rain-filled irrigation tank for watering plantings on the property.
13. Encourage people to use alternate means of travel to gather at your building. Aim for a parking lot that has as many bicycles as cars. (Let it be known that in connection with this idea, casual clothing would be accepted and considered appropriate.)

D. *Congregational Education*

1. Make use of books and articles in your church library that focus on creation care for different age groups.

2. Identify your church's connection to its environment by answering questions like these: What materials make up the products that we use? Where does our food come from? Where does our waste go?
3. Hold a six- or seven-week mini-series to explain the degradations of creation. Most people are unaware of the *actual* problems. Some sessions could be used to develop ideas for righting the wrongs that have been identified.
4. Provide pastors and teachers an opportunity to complete a special course of study dealing with responsibility to God's creation.
5. Develop service projects that involve families: flower and tree planting, recycling programs, adopting a highway stewardship program, speaking to area churches about stewardship.
6. Serve as a host for children from an inner-city church for a week. Focus together on the wonders of God's creation, aiming to learn from each other.
7. Involve church members in activities that support local agricultural efforts in soil stewardship, such as contour cropping, intensive rotational grazing, reduced chemical inputs, and improved animal care.
8. Fund and support members of your church to act as environmental stewards to debate and influence public policy in the interest of maintaining and restoring creation's integrity.

E. *Stewardship Education for Congregation and Community*

1. Invite people in your community to be part of your Creation Care Center.
2. Offer community education classes on the how, what, and where of recycling and energy conservation in your area. Become an information center for source reduction and all kinds of recycling.
3. Provide information on environmentally sound practices, such as the efficient use of home thermostats, air conditioners, and coffee makers; the safe disposal of home cleansers, batteries, plastics, petroleum-based products, organic matter—and so on.
4. Make an inventory of all plant and animal communities within a half-mile radius of your church. Display this inventory pictorially as an exhibit.
5. Organize annual or semi-annual "Creation Rehabilitation Workdays" for planting trees, cleaning up a stretch of highway, landscaping a vacant lot, or buying some land and protecting it.
6. Reclaim a piece of land—an urban park, a city block, or some other area, and take care of it, modeling stewardship and involving area residents. Or adopt a wetland or woodland, keeping it, caring for it, and using it to educate yourselves and others.
7. Take a field trip to a local landfill to show people the waste we generate in our society.

F. Study Groups, Youth, and Christian Education

1. With the others in your church, approach Bible study with an openness to receive the message of the Creator on creation care and keeping.
2. Hold vacation Bible school at a local county park, or hold the final celebration of the Bible school at a park, hosting a potluck dinner afterward. Bring students on walks for the purpose of discovering creation, learning awe and wonder, and developing an understanding of caring for creation.
3. Start an environmental awareness and creation care program with Sunday school students, involving them in an environmental cleanup or appreciation project each month.
4. Make creation awareness part of the church school curriculum. Involve adults of all ages in teaching lessons for the children about the need to preserve our world, and provide practical instruction in how to do this. Help children understand animals through pets under their care.
5. Gather a forum of interested business and science professionals in your church or wider community to discuss and propose solutions for alternative energy sources, renewable energy concepts, and improved energy use in support of creation care and keeping.

G. Congregational Life and Response to Creation

1. As a congregation, commit to living out your faith through caring for the part of God's creation in which you live. For example, commit to caring for a nearby creek or watershed, adopting a highway or endangered species, recycling the garbage you produce, and keeping your cars and homes as environmentally fit as possible.
2. Arrange for informal meetings of church families at a local park on a regular basis. Invite individuals who can give presentations on nature to help people notice and understand their natural surroundings.
3. Start a program that involves all family members in conducting whole-family environmental and conservation projects in and around their homes and neighborhoods.
4. Have each individual set a personal goal each month to transform talk into action.
5. Hold a Friday- or Saturday-evening retreat that includes nature study and star-watching.
6. Plan a multigenerational tree-planting event that involves entire families.

H. Resource Use and Conservation

1. Purchase glass or ceramic dinnerware and communion cups instead of throwaway paper and plastic products.
2. Arrange to have various meetings held at the same time to conserve heat and air conditioning.
3. Adopt a "no chemical use" policy for lawn and plant care.

4. Adopt a "no throwaway" policy for functions at which food and drinks are served.
5. Use cloth tablecloths for church functions.
6. Use recycled paper for church bulletins, publications, and correspondence.
7. Put timers on outside lights.
8. Put motion- and light-detecting wall switches in appropriate places so that lights automatically go out when people are not present or when natural lighting is adequate.
9. Develop a car pool or mass-transit arrangement for bringing members to church. Also include bicycle racks. This will reduce the need for a large parking lot and will allow you to turn part of it into a garden for trees, flowers, and other plants.

I. Personal Lives, Lifestyle, and Home
1. Encourage members to make their homes and workplaces into Creation Care Centers.
2. Provide opportunities for all members to commit themselves to stating what they will do as stewards of creation.
3. Arrange for a "pedal-power activity" and use it as a basis for discussing how you can help others, yourselves, and creation.
4. Adopt energy-efficient practices for the use of heaters, air conditioners, lights, and various appliances at home.
5. Continue to be a witness to others through the example of creation care displayed in your own life.

J. Cooperation with Other Churches
1. Invite two or three nearby churches to join you in forming a Creation Care Center. Publicize what you are doing to encourage others.
2. Form a team to glean from other churches the best ideas and approaches for making your church a Creation Care Center, and present these concepts to your church leaders to stimulate thinking and response.
3. Plan a community-wide workshop on God's creation that involves all the churches of the community. Follow up with projects on energy conservation, clean-up, materials use, and more.
4. Conduct a city-wide energy and waste audit of church buildings.

K. Providing Leadership in Society
1. Be leaders in speaking out against the degradation of creation.
2. Continue efforts with other churches in the community to form a task force to encourage concern about environmental issues, and work on things that the community as a whole can do to improve or properly take care of the environment (such as cleaning up a riverbank, lakeshore, or part of a highway).

3. Conduct a study of various occupations and how they affect creation, and then discuss these issues in a community forum, inviting businesses and workers and others to brainstorm about how to improve on or eliminate negative impacts.
4. Urge your church's local or governing body, or even the church universal, to make a statement about creation and the environment that offers practical application for daily living.

L. Yet More Ideas!

- Build window boxes, rooftop gardens, ground-level gardens; promote other environmentally conscious architecture.
- Build fish ponds with fluorescent night lights for insect feeding.
- Plant edible flowers (nasturtiums).
- Encourage or practice rotational grazing or regenerative gardening.
- Engage in native plant restoration, indigenous gardening, and forest garden techniques.
- Encourage seed and tree distribution.
- Reclaim creation terminology in liturgy, psalmody, hymnody, and sermons.
- Establish walking trails through woodlands, fields, and gardens; include signs that identify tree and plant varieties.
- Restore habitats around homes to provide for a large diversity of creatures.
- Develop lawns with biodiversity that fix their own atmospheric nitrogen and naturally recycle thatch.
- Assist on a farm; buy the beef you eat "on the hoof" and have it processed.
- Purchase a hundred acres of tropical rainforest for preservation.
- Give environmental stewardship awards to deserving members of the community.
- Develop a paid summer stewardship mission experience for young people at the wages they might earn as a fast-food clerk.
- Make your church a distribution center for native flowers and trees on Arbor Day.
- Make your church a distribution center for vegetable seeds and related literature on food and the environment in late spring.
- Talk with a farmer about planting a crop for direct human consumption; help identify a market for it; direct any surplus food to a local food pantry.
- Develop a wheelchair nature loop at a retirement or nursing home.
- Conduct a food-source or hunger awareness dinner at church.
- Encourage a local restaurant to use placemats that show the relationship of menu items to the places where food is grown.
- Encourage a local newspaper to get involved in environmental issues.
- Organize the restoration of native vegetation along a stretch of roadside.

- Discuss the difference between tree planting and forest restoration and follow it with a restoration project.
- Buy a worn-out piece of land and redeem it for productive gardening or re-establishment of native species.
- Arrange for an "astronomy night" to help make Psalm 19 come alive.
- Spend a half-hour or more in autumn lying on a forest floor, listening to leaves fall and observing woodland creatures.

Suggestions for Group Session

GETTING STARTED

This chapter provides a fresh twist in our study by giving us ideas on doing something practical and important for the good of God's creation. We have come to the point where we can take what we have learned about creation care and develop a practical response. This response will help us specify how we can begin making our church, household, or larger community into a Creation Care Center.

Scripture Reading
Psalm 96

Opening Prayer
Pray that your church, household, and larger community will become more aware of creation and make practical changes in order to serve God and creation more faithfully in thought, word, and deed. Pray that we might always conduct our lives in such a way that we image God's love for creation.

DISCUSSION AND ACTIVITY

We suggest that the group follow the mini-workshop procedure outlined near the beginning of this chapter; it will take up most, if not all, of your session time.

After using the notecard procedure, invite everyone to skim the pages of additional ideas presented in this chapter. The group may want to add some of these ideas to the ones they've already included in the stacks of notecards. Please be sure to appoint a subgroup to do the necessary follow-up of cataloging, writing, and report distribution.

Option: In place of using notecards during this session, you could devise another system for generating and recording ideas. For example, you could use a dry-erase marker board or overhead transparencies. Compile these ideas into a document that can be distributed later.

Optional Procedure
For an option to the mini-workshop procedure outlined earlier, your group may instead wish to do the following:

- Skim the lists of creation care ideas supplied in this chapter, placing a checkmark next to those that could work well for your congregation.
- Share all checked ideas with the entire group.
- Add other ideas that group members generate.
- Go back through each category and decide which ideas you could actually implement.
- Appoint a subgroup to write up and distribute your findings along with an action plan.

Thank the group for their helpful contributions, noting the depth and breadth of interest represented in the ideas.

Scripture Discussion

Group members may also want to discuss one or more of the following questions:

1. Read Psalm 96. How does the psalmist portray the earth—as a living thing or as an inanimate thing? Explain.

2. Select one or two phrases from Psalm 96 and explain why you enjoy them.

3. What is Psalm 96 really about—creation or God? Can the world in its present condition really praise God? Explain. Share one or two other favorite passages about God's work and power in creation and how creation glorifies God.

CLOSING

Give thanks to God for the testimony of the Scriptures and the testimony of all that God has made. Give thanks too for the minds with which our Creator has endowed us and for the ideas we have generated and chosen using this marvelous gift. Ask God's blessing on those who will compile the results of this session, and pray for the whole body of Christ in its calling to live responsibly in creation.

SIX

Clearing Away Obstacles to Positive Action

In chapter 1 of this book we nurtured our awe and wonder of God as our amazing Creator, the Maker of heaven and earth and all provisions of creation. But then we were confronted with the ongoing and accelerating degradation of the earth that in many ways results from human abuse of God's provisions. We then responded by searching the Scriptures and identifying and reflecting on many marvelous teachings on creation care. We also made use of what we learned in order to generate an organized list of specific ideas for action. Now we are ready to act on what we know and believe! But there may yet be a few obstacles to clear away before we begin.

We know there are lots of things we should do in life, including taking care of the creation God has given us. But often we just don't do many of the things we know we should do. In many cases, there are reasons for this. Some things get in our way and make us stumble—so much so that we might never get past "square one." Also there can be such big holes in the road that they not only give us a jolt but open up to consume us—such that our intended journey stops abruptly before we get to where we were going.

In this concluding chapter, then, let's identify some stumbling blocks that may prevent us from taking action, and then we'll look at a major pitfall we'll want to avoid so that we don't get swallowed up along the path of creation stewardship. Having done this, we will be ready to put our beliefs into practice.

STUMBLING BLOCKS TO CREATION CARE AND KEEPING

There are quite a number of troublesome stumbling blocks in the way of creation-keeping discipleship. Some of these we have invented ourselves; others have been devised by our friends; still others have been devised by enemies.

What are these stumbling blocks? Here are some common ones along with comments that may help us in removing or avoiding these obstacles.

This world is not my home; I'm just passing through. (Translation: *Since we are headed for heaven anyway, why take care of creation?*)

It's true that people who truly believe in Jesus Christ receive the gift of ever-lasting life. But everlasting life in Christ includes the here-and-now, in which we take care of our teeth, our hair, and all other parts of our body. We also take care of our possessions—clothes, automobiles, homes, and so on. We do all this even though "our days may come to seventy years, or eighty, if our strength endures" (Ps. 90:10). Have you ever wondered if perhaps learning how to take care of things in this part of eternity might be important for the care of things we will be entrusted with later? The world we live in is much more enduring than our selves or our possessions. So shouldn't the care of creation also be a part of our here-and-now concern? (Review the closing paragraphs of chapter 4.)

Caring for creation gets us too close to the New Age movement. (Translation: *I don't want people to think I'm a New Ager. Isn't concern for the environment and working for a better world what New Age is all about?*)

For thousands of years now, believers have looked forward to the coming of the kingdom of God, and that includes the renewal of God's created world (Rom. 8:19-22; Rev. 21-22). As we have noted in earlier chapters, the Bible also makes clear that human beings are earth's caretakers (Gen. 1:27-30; 2:15). As Christians, we confess that our entire earth belongs to God. It is not the private property of any group.

Respecting creation gets us too close to pantheism. (Translation: *If you care for plants and animals, and especially if you value protecting endangered species, you are close to worshiping them as gods.*)

Surprisingly, pantheism (the belief that God is in all things and that all things are in God) is a growing problem even in our scientific age. In our study of creation, we must be careful to worship the Creator, not the creation; we must be clear in conveying the good news that God is the Creator, Sustainer, and Redeemer and that the awe and wonder we develop from the study of creation is praise for the Maker of all things. But this does not mean we may avoid taking care of creation. The example of Noah is instructive: Noah cared for the creatures on the ark, preserving all the species endangered by the flood—not because they were gods but because God required it (Gen. 7:13-16).

We need to avoid anything that looks like political correctness. (Translation: *Being "politically correct" these days means being pro-abortion and pro-environment, and I'll have nothing to do with that.*)

The Ku Klux Klan, a racist organization in the United States, uses the symbol of the cross in its terrorizing activities. Does this mean that Christians no longer should use the symbol of the cross in their churches? Some alternative religious and lifestyle groups use the symbol of the rainbow in their literature. Does this mean that Christians should stop using this symbol in their educational materials? People who identify themselves as "politically correct" may advocate for saving uneconomic species from extinction. Does this mean that Christians should not act to preserve God's living creatures? We approach the subject of caring for creation as God's stewards, not as members of a politically correct group.

There are too many worldly people out there doing environmental things. (Translation: *If people who don't share my beliefs in God and Jesus Christ are working to save the earth, I know it can't be right for me.*)

In Isaiah 45:1-6 we read that unbelieving Cyrus was anointed to do God's work. Often if God's people are unwilling or unable to do God's work, God sees to it that the work gets done anyway. So if there are some worldly people out there clearly doing God's work, let's be glad for the help and not use this fact to excuse ourselves from our God-given task as stewards of God's creation.

Caring for creation will lead to world government. (Translation: *If we try to tackle global environmental problems, we'll have to cooperate with other nations, and that will help set the stage for world government.*)

There is no doubt that cooperation (with unbelievers and with other nations) will be necessary in order to address many environmental concerns. Migrating birds, for example, do not recognize international boundaries. Their care may involve the cooperation of many nations along their migratory path. Such cooperation does not have to lead to world government. For example, the work of the International Crane Foundation to care for wetland habitats and birds has been accomplished through cooperation between Russia and China and between North Korea and South Korea. The end result has not been a merging of these nation's governments.

Before you know it, we will have to support abortion. (Translation: *Because of the relationship between environmental degradation and growing human popula-*

tion, we will soon find ourselves having to accept abortion as a solution to environmental problems.)

Our obligation and privilege to care for God's creation does not give us license to use any means at our disposal to address environmental problems. The fact that many people justify abortion as a population-growth control does not mean that people who are convicted of a God-given responsibility of stewardship should not work to care for the earth, including its population problems.

I don't want to be an extremist or alarmist. (Translation: *I want to be considered normal and not some kind of prophet of gloom and doom.*)

Gloom and doom are not necessary components of the message about caring for creation. Frightening ourselves into action is far less preferable than caring for creation out of gratitude and love for God. As for being called an alarmist, is it wrong to sound the fire alarm when a building is burning? In many cases today it may be necessary to sound the alarm.

Dominion over creation means oppressive domination. (Translation: *I think the Bible says we have the right to destroy things that get in our way; that's what dominion is all about.*)

Many critics of the Bible have pointed to Genesis 1:28 (in the King James and Revised Standard versions, among others, which translate *radahl* as "have dominion") to show that it is the root cause of environmental problems. But dominion as outright oppression is not advocated or condoned by Scripture. First, Genesis 1:28 gives the blessing and mandate to people *before the fall into sin.* Second, this passage must be understood not in isolation but in the context of the rest of the Bible, which shows that dominion means responsible stewardship. Having dominion over creation is an important aspect of being made in God's image. Part of our human dignity is tied to God's entrusting us with stewardship over creation.

People are more important than the environment. (Translation: *I'm for people, and that means that people are more important than saving species of plants and animals. If anything is endangered, it is people, not Furbish louseworts or snail darters.*)

We often hear this rationalization for not saving living species threatened with extinction. But again we must ask, "What does the Bible teach?" Recall the account of the flood in Genesis 6-9. Who perishes? Who is saved? Are species less important than individual people? At the very least, care for living species cannot be disregarded because of the importance of people. Christ's redemption covers all creation, not just humans.

We must tell "both sides" of environmental issues. (Translation: *There are always two sides to an argument, so if my own views against environmentalism are being attacked, I should be able to find support to protect my interests.*)

There is present among us a concerted effort to promote doubt and uncertainty whenever it helps maintain sinful structures and institutions fueled mainly by greed. The most familiar of such efforts is that of the tobacco industry, which, even after extensive and conclusive evidence showing that smoking produces lung cancer and other health concerns, has sustained a campaign that confuses the issues and maintains distrust of cancer research. As a result, this powerful industry protects its markets for a product that degrades and destroys the human body. Similar efforts have been expanded with high levels of funding support to discredit the science of climatology and its findings on global climate change. A major strategy for promoting the discredit of science is to seek any contrary opinions, dress them up in scientific garb, and put them on display and in debate with the findings of science.

Science is necessarily suspect. (Translation: *Science teaches atheism, and because I am against atheism I also am against science.*)

Promoters of doubt about the findings of climatology and environmental science have become expert in playing on the fears and apprehensions of the public. In so doing they have discovered that linking science with the question of the origins of life and with evolution will cast a pall on all science, regardless of whether it has to do with origins or evolution. The result is an assault on science as a principal way of learning how the world works. The integrity of science that pursues knowledge about the world is based on careful statements of findings, including uncertainties. This tentativeness of science—which is one of its principal features—is preyed upon by detractors to discredit this highly disciplined and remarkably credible truth-seeking enterprise. In addition, many influential scientists are committed Christians.

A PITFALL TO CREATION CARE AND KEEPING

Beyond the stumbling blocks we have noted, there are also pitfalls that can prevent us from becoming stewards of our Lord's creation. One of these is particularly effective and can seriously mislead and trap us, making us believe we are doing the real thing while eroding and damaging our own life and our ability to be stewards of God's earth.

Across Christendom there is a widely held belief in two major revelations through which we come to know God: special revelation and natural (or general) revelation. Special revelation is the revelation of God in Scripture, the Bible, made up of both the Old and New Testaments. Natural revelation is the revelation of God in the creation—the entire created universe of which we are a part. Through natural

81

revelation we discover that God is the author of creation. We could call the created world and the written Word the "two books" of God's revelation.

Most Christians affirm this "two-book" approach to divine revelation. But there have always been some "one-book" Christians who have seen the Bible, or special revelation, as the only way by which God reveals himself to us. They usually do not remain "one-book" Christians for long because the Bible itself affirms general revelation (Ps. 19:1; Acts 14:17; Rom. 1:20).

Some people, however, who are familiar with parts of the Bible and perhaps have grown up in Jewish or Christian communities, have become so impressed with the natural sciences and how the world works that they have come to believe the natural world is the only revelation that has ultimate meaning. They too have become "one-book" people. Some who believe this way consider themselves "post-Christian." They acknowledge their roots and their "journey" through Christianity, but they see themselves as having passed through such thinking. Some of these "one-book" believers see the Bible as a major stumbling block to living rightly on the earth today, and they insist that the Bible should be dismissed as totally irrelevant.

Many of these "one-book" believers confess an "earth-centered spirituality" that they think should replace the teachings of the Bible. For example, they want to replace the word *God* with the world *Reality* and speak of the *kingdom of God* as the *reign of reality.* This kind of thinking denies the authority of the Bible and the reality of a personal God.

"One-book" believers who advocate creation-centered spirituality often describe God as something that emerges from the world as a developing consciousness. For them, God is an expression of the evolutionary unfolding of the universe. Christ has been transformed into the "Christ Spirit" that is somehow the expression of the earth's spiritual nature.

The pitfall here is not so much that there is a developing belief around earth-centered spirituality. The pitfall is that such thinking can easily infiltrate the church. Adherents to this philosophy believe that it is needed in the church. They see it as necessary for weaning Christianity away from its trust in the Bible and in the personal God of Abraham, Isaac, and Jacob. They feel that believers must be weaned from trusting in Jesus Christ as Lord. They want to bring the church to the maturity that comes through the new light shed by the revelation of the earth itself.

But God provides some remarkably easy means for avoiding this pitfall:

- Continue to pray to God our Father in the name of Jesus Christ.
- Continue to read and believe God's written Word.
- Continue to be willing to be led by the Holy Spirit in our daily walk.

People who are fully committed to earth spirituality cannot do these things because that undermines their "religion." Such people deny the power of the Scriptures to inform us; they deny that we have access through prayer to God who, through our Mediator, Jesus Christ, can hear and respond to our concerns and petitions; and they deny that the Holy Spirit has power in this world to guide us. While we must be compassionate to all who seek to care for God's creation, we must also equip ourselves with the power of God's Word to do the work that needs to be done.

NOW WHAT MUST WE DO?

What must we do about creation? The simple yet profound response to this question is this: "Love God as Redeemer *and* Creator, acknowledge God's love for all creation, and act upon this by following Jesus—the one who redeems, upholds, reconciles, and rules all things."

But a serious problem remains: because of human sin, most people have been alienated from the Creator and creation. It is difficult to love, uphold, and care for a world that we really do not know. Thus many will first have to become aware of creation and its God-declared goodness. As believers in Christ, we are called to share this good news and invite others to come to know the one true personal God and Savior.

Once people are aware of God and his love for his creation (including us!), we can move on to appreciation and stewardship. So we have this framework to describe our response:

- Awareness (seeing, identifying, naming, locating)
- Appreciation (tolerating, respecting, valuing, esteeming, cherishing)
- Stewardship (using, restoring, serving, keeping, entrusting)

Our ultimate purpose is to honor God as Creator in such a way that Christian environmental stewardship is part and parcel of everything we do. Our goal is to make tending the garden of creation, in all its aspects, an unquestioned and all-pervasive part of our service to each other, to our community, to God's world.

Let's deal briefly with each of the three steps, as follows.

Awareness

In a time when so much calls for our attention—international affairs, local politics, our work or schooling, family needs, church commitments, and other busyness—we might only barely notice the natural and environmental aspects of creation in our surroundings. We might take time to notice and learn things about creation only when we have a day off or when we take a vacation trip—and even then our impressions may be seriously obscured. We must consciously make ourselves aware of what is happening in God's creation.

Awareness involves seeing, naming, identifying, and locating different parts of God's creation. It means taking off blinders that we or society may put on us to keep us focused on our pursuits in life. It means providing ourselves with enough quiet, reflection, and learning time that we can notice and identify a tree or mountain, bird or river. It means entering the natural world intentionally in order to locate and find God's creatures that we sing about in a favorite doxology: "Praise God . . . all creatures here below."

Appreciation

From awareness comes appreciation; we cannot appreciate something we are unaware of. At the very least, appreciation means tolerating what we are aware of. We may tolerate, for example, worms and hyenas. But appreciation can also involve respect. We certainly respect a large bear, but we can also develop respect for a lowly worm as we learn of its critical importance to the rest of creation. We can move, as well, from toleration to respect to valuing. The earth and everything in it has value because God made it so. As we become aware of the order of creation, we will image God's valuing of all his works. And this will build even further until we even esteem and cherish much of what we discover.

Stewardship

Appreciation needs to lead to stewardship. Stewardship takes us beyond appreciation to restoration. We now work for the restoration of what has been degraded in the past.

Beyond restoration, stewardship means serving. As we understand that God through creation is in so many ways serving us, we grow to willingly return this service with our own. This service includes a loving and caring keeping of what God has given us to hold in trust. And our service in creation will eventually involve entrusting others with what we have served, kept, and restored.

Christian environmental stewardship—our loving care and keeping of creation—is a central, joyful part of the human task. As communities of God's stewards—as the worldwide body of the one who redeems and reconciles all things—our churches and our lives can and must be vibrant testimonies to our Redeemer and Creator.

"You are worthy, our Lord and God, to receive glory and honor
and power, for you created all things, and by your will they were
created and have their being."

—*Revelation 4:11*

Suggestions for Group Session

GETTING STARTED

Through this book we have discovered what we can do in our church, household, and community to care for God's creation, and now we have to face up to a very real problem. We can be easily distracted and sidetracked from putting what we know into practice. This chapter explores some aspects of this problem by discussing stumbling blocks and pitfalls, and this gives us an opportunity to explore our own reasons for not acting. As a result, this chapter aims to help us clear the way to act on our beliefs as stewards of our Lord's creation, to the praise and glory of our Creator.

Scripture Readings
Ezekiel 33:1-20
Romans 7:15-25
Ephesians 4:14-24
James 1:22-25
Revelation 4:11

Opening Prayer
Pray that all of us in the body of Christ may be inspired to be faithful stewards of God's creation without getting sidetracked or tripped up by distractions. Pray for the ability to discern what is right. Pray for others too, that they might not be misled but rather guided to acknowledge and respect their Creator in thought and word and in concrete, meaningful actions.

FOR DISCUSSION

How should we understand ourselves and others?

1. Why don't we always do what we believe we should do? Given what we have read in this chapter, and thinking through what you know from Scripture, ask and discuss this question: "Why is it that so often we don't do what we know we should, and we do what we know we shouldn't?" (See Romans 7:15-25.)

2. How do we relate to people whose beliefs are different from ours? New Age, relativism, pantheism, political correctness, worldly environmentalism—the list goes on. Given the true teachings of the Bible, how are we expected to relate to people who believe differently than we do? Do we have any responsibility toward them? Explain.

3. How can we deal with environmental problems that require cooperation with people from other nations and other faiths? Should we cooperate with others on these matters? Can we preserve our own faith in the process? Should we? What must we do?

How should we regard other obstacles?

4. What about population? Do Christians have to be concerned with the number of people on earth? With the consumption per person? Why or why not?

5. What do we do with alarmists and prophets of gloom and doom? Prophets and prophecy occur throughout the Scriptures. What does the Bible teach us about the importance of prophets? Were any of them alarmists? What does Ezekiel 33:1-20 tell us, and is this at all relevant for us today? Why or why not?

6. What about dominion? Douglas John Hall wrote a book titled *Imaging God: Dominion as Service*. From what we have learned together, explain the meaning of this title. Consider also the title of a book by Matthew Scully: *Dominion: The Power of Man, the Suffering of Animals, and the Call to Mercy*. Some of you may have read these books. If so, what's your opinion of them? Have they helped you better understand our role in creation? Explain.

7. What is discernment? In view of stumbling blocks and pitfalls along the road to stewardship, discuss the importance of discernment in our daily walk.

How will we now respond?
8. Now what must we do? What is the difference between awareness, appreciation, and stewardship? Can you have stewardship without awareness? Without appreciation? Explain.

9. Do we merely listen to God's Word, or do we also do what it says? Read James 1:22-25. How can we apply this passage to environmental issues?

10. What's the next step in our implementation plan? By now, you probably have the organized results of your mini-workshop on creation care (chap. 5). Remind each other of the next step that needs to be taken, and commit together to follow through on your important work.

CLOSING

Pray together for God's continued leading; pray to be disciples of the one through whom the world was made and in whom it is held together and reconciled. Give thanks to God for creation, and pray that the Holy Spirit will lead each group member to action. Also give thanks for the church of Jesus Christ, praying that its members throughout the world will eagerly serve as the children of God for whom the whole creation waits with eager expectation (Rom. 8:19).

Postscript

Dear Reader,

I hope that this book has been mostly inspiring and uplifting to you. I hope it has helped empower you and your friends to address the world and its environmental concerns in a healthy, wholesome way—in your church, community, and household. I also hope you have renewed with me your awe and wonder for our Lord's creation.

Earlier in this book you probably also experienced the stress that I have felt, having to face up to human degradation of creation and its roots in human sinfulness. But we have now passed through that valley and have come to the highland of participation in the joy and delight of responding in love and gratitude to the Creator of heaven and earth. We have entered the light of imaging God's care for creation. We are affirmed now in our deep-seated hope that God's creatures of whom we sing will continue their successive generations of praise to God.

Today I sit again at the edge of the great Waubesa Marsh—the magnificent masterpiece of which I am a steward. And as they have been doing here every year for thousands of years, the returning cranes are again clangoring in wild song! "Praise God . . . all creatures here below!" May they continue to praise God through the coming generations. And may the Lord bless and keep you, as together we continue to keep our Lord's earth!

—Cal DeWitt, 2007

Resources

Belgic Confession. Grand Rapids, Mich.: CRC Publications, 1985.

Berry, R. J., ed. *The Care of Creation: Focusing Concern and Action*. Leicester, Eng.: InterVarsity, 2000.

Berry, R. J., ed. *Environmental Stewardship: Critical Perspectives—Past and Present*. London: T&T Clark, 2006.

Berry, Wendell. *The Unsettling of America: Culture and Agriculture*. New York: Avon, 1977.

Bouma-Prediger, Steven. *For the Beauty of the Earth: A Christian Vision for Creation Care*. Grand Rapids, Mich.: Baker, 2001.

Bratton, Susan P. *Six Billion and More: Human Population Regulation and Christian Ethics*. Louisville, Ky.: John Knox/Westminster Press, 1992.

Brueggemann, Walter. *The Land: Place as Gift, Promise, and Challenge in Biblical Faith*. Second ed. Philadelphia: Fortress, 2002.

Cahill, Thomas. *How the Irish Saved Civilization: The Untold Story of Ireland's Heroic Role from the Fall of Rome to the Rise of Medieval Europe*. New York: Nan A. Talese, Doubleday, 1995, 1996.

Calvin, John. *Commentary on Genesis*, 1554 (from the English translation of 1847, as reprinted by Banner of Truth Publishers, Edinburgh, Scotland, 1965).

Daly, Herman E. and Kenneth N. Townsend, eds. *Valuing the Earth: Economics, Ecology, Ethics*. Cambridge, Mass.: MIT Press, 1993.

DeWitt, Calvin B., ed. *The Environment and the Christian: What Can We Learn from the New Testament?* Grand Rapids, Mich.: Baker, 1991.

DeWitt, Calvin B. and Ghillean T. Prance, eds. *Missionary Earthkeeping*. Macon, Ga.: Mercer University Press, 1992.

DeWitt, Calvin B. *Caring for Creation: Responsible Stewardship of God's Handiwork*. Grand Rapids, Mich.: Baker, 1998.

Farley, Joshua and Herman E. Daly. *Ecological Economics: Principles and Applications*. Washington, D.C.: Island Press, 2001.

Freudenberger, C. Dean. *Global Dust Bowl: Can We Stop the Destruction of the Land Before It's Too Late?* Minneapolis: Augsburg, 1988.

Granberg-Michaelson, Wesley, ed. *Tending the Garden: Essays on the Gospel and the Earth*. Grand Rapids, Mich: Eerdmans, 1987.

Hall, Douglas John. *Imaging God: Dominion as Stewardship*. Grand Rapids, Mich.: Eerdmans, 1986.

Houghton, John T. *Global Warming: The Complete Briefing*. Third ed. Cambridge: Cambridge University Press, 2004.

Meyer, Art and Jocele. *Earthkeepers: Environmental Perspectives on Hunger, Poverty, and Injustice*. Scottdale, Pa., and Waterloo, Ont.: Herald Press, 1991.

Psalter Hymnal. Grand Rapids, Mich.: Board of Publications of the Christian Reformed Church, 1959, 1976.

Psalter Hymnal. Grand Rapids, Mich.: CRC Publications, 1987, 1988.

Scully, Matthew. *Dominion: The Power of Man, the Suffering of Animals, and the Call to Mercy*. New York: St. Martin's, 2002.

Wright, Richard T. and Bernard J. Nebel. *Environmental Science: Toward a Sustainable Future*. Tenth ed. Englewood Cliffs, N.J.: Prentice Hall, 2007.

Vischer, Lukas. *Caring for God's Creation: A Challenge for the Church's Mission*. Geneva: John Knox Series, 2007.

Wilkinson, Loren, ed. *Earthkeeping in the Nineties: Stewardship of Creation*. Grand Rapids, Mich.: Eerdmans, 1991.

Young's Literal Translation of the Bible: A Revised Edition. Grand Rapids, Mich.: Baker, 1953.

NEWSPAPERS AND JOURNALS TO READ

Christian Science Monitor

Nature

Science

Bioscience

Credits

The chapters in this book are based upon the following papers and articles by the author.

CHAPTER ONE

"God's Love for the World and Creation's Environmental Challenge to Evangelical Christianity." *Evangelical Review of Theology* 17(2):134-149; 1993.

"Creation's Environmental Challenge to Evangelical Christianity" in R. J. Berry, ed., *The Care of Creation: Focusing Concern and Action*. Leicester, Eng.: InterVarsity, 2000; pp. 60-73.

CHAPTER TWO

"Seven Degradations of Creation." *Perspectives* 3(2):4-8; 1989.

"Assaulting the Gallery of God: Humanity's Seven Degradations of the Earth." *Sojourners* 19(2):19-21; 1990.

"Biogeographic and Trophic Restructuring of the Biosphere: The State of the Earth Under Human Domination." *Christian Scholar's Review* 32:347-364; 2003.

CHAPTER THREE

"Respecting Creation's Integrity: Biblical Principles for Environmental Responsibility." *Firmament* 3(3):10-11, 20-21; 1992.

"Biblical Principles and Environmental Ethics." *Environmental Review* 3(10):10-16; 1996.

"Christianity: Biblical Foundations for Christian Stewardship" in Bron Taylor, ed., *The Encyclopedia of Religion and Nature*, 2005.

CHAPTER FOUR

"Creation's Care and Keeping: A Reformed Perspective." *Theological Forum* (Reformed Ecumenical Council) 19(4):1-7; 1991.

"Ecology and Ethics: Relation of Religious Belief to Ecological Practice in the Biblical Tradition." *Biodiversity and Conservation* 4:838-848; 1995. Also published in N. S. Cooper and R. C. J. Carling, eds., *Ecologists and Ethical Judgments,* London: Chapman & Hall, 1996.

"Behemoth and Batrachians in the Eye of God: Responsibility to Other Kinds in Biblical Perspective" in Dieter T. Hessel and Rosemary Radford Ruether, eds., *Christianity and Ecology: Seeking the Well-Being of Earth and Humans*, Cambridge: Harvard Univ. Press, 2000; pp. 291-316.

"The Place of Creation in Today's Missionary Discourse" in Lukas Vischer, *Caring for God's Creation: A Challenge for the Church's Mission,* Geneva: John Knox Series, 2007.

"Contemporary Missiology and the Biosphere" in Daniel Jeyaraj, Robert W. Pazmio, and Rodney Petersen, eds., *Antioch Agenda: Essays on the Restorative Church in Honor of Orlando E. Costas*, New Delhi: Indian Society for the Promotion of Christian Knowledge, 2007; pp. 305-328.

"To Safeguard and Renew: The Principles of Stewardship of the Creation" in Andrew Walls and Cathy Ross, eds., *Mission in the Twenty-First Century: Exploring the Five Marks of Global Mission,* London: Darton, Longman, and Todd, 2008.

CHAPTER FIVE

"Making Your Church a Creation Awareness Center" in Donna Lehman, *What on Earth Can You Do: Making Your Church a Creation Awareness Center*, Scottdale, Pa., and Waterloo, Ont.: Herald Press, 1993; pp. 169-191 (Appendix A).

"Ideas of University of Wisconsin-Madison Students" in Donna Lehman, *What on Earth Can You Do: Making Your Church a Creation Awareness Center*, Scottdale, Pa., and Waterloo, Ont.: Herald Press, 1993; pp. 192-195 (Appendix B).

"Christian Environmental Stewardship: Preparing the Way for Action." *Perspectives on Science and Christian Faith* 46:80-89; 1994.

"You Can Make Your Church a Creation Awareness Center!" *Green Cross* 1(2):12-15; 1995.

"Behold the Birds of the Air! The Educational Importance of Environmental Awareness." *Christian Educators Journal,* 2002.

"Climate Care: Our Profound Moral Imperative." *The Banner* 142(4):18-20; 2007.

CHAPTER SIX

"God's Love for the World and Creation's Environmental Challenge to Evangelical Christianity." *Evangelical Review of Theology* 17(2):134-149; 1993.

"Creation and God's Judgment." *Perspectives on Science and Christian Faith* 48(Sept.):182-183; 1996.

"Creation's Environmental Challenge to Evangelical Christianity" in R. J. Berry, ed., *The Care of Creation: Focusing Concern and Action.* Leicester, Eng.: InterVarsity, 2000; pp. 60-73.